Praise for *Unrepeatable*

"From first page to last, this is a book rich in three vital ways: a keen grasp of our current culture, its challenges and what to do about them; excellent counsel on the nature and skills of mentoring; and a passion for awakening the unrepeatable vocation of every Christian soul. Beautifully written, compellingly personal, and a treasure to read."

MOST REV. CHARLES J. CHAPUT, O.F.M. CAP.
Archbishop of Philadelphia

"This spiritually grounded, easy-to-read treatise is a solid piece of research, and yet, is still packed throughout with supporting anecdotes that the reader will recognize and appreciate. Eminently practicable, *Unrepeatable: Cultivating the Unique Calling of Every Person* is for every Christian, especially the teacher, counselor, or spiritual director who is truly serious about sifting through the cultural morass to find the 'right' vocation, rather than just a job."

MOST. REV. ROBERT BARRON
Auxiliary Bishop, Archdiocese of Los Angeles,
and Founder of Word on Fire Catholic Ministries

"The work of Luke Burgis and Joshua Miller is a welcome and necessary fresh approach to the rich tradition of vocational discernment. They break open the stale and entrenched idea of a precast decision dependent on God alone that requires one to figure it out like a puzzle. Through story and metaphor, relying on the wisdom of spiritual masters, sound philosophy and theology, along with examples in pop culture, they demonstrate that every person has a vocation. And it is found in the form of a 'story': a person's own story. *Unrepeatable* is written in an engaging style that will appeal to young searching hearts. It will also serve vocation directors, mentors, coaches, and all people who are serious about being equipped to accompany young people to ask the right questions on their journey of self-discovery, finding their mission, and ultimately their vocation 'back to the heart of God.' I enthusiastically encourage this book as a means to help foster a new culture of vocational discernment."

MOST REV. JAMES F. CHECCHIO
Former Rector of the Pontifical North American College and Bishop of Metuchen, New Jersey

"Luke and Joshua use the power of narrative to tell the story of stories: the story of the happiness that Jesus Christ has brought us. In an amenable style they convey deep thoughts taken from the treasure of Catholic faith. I recommend this book as a guide on your own individual path of vocation."

MSGR. MARTIN SCHLAG
Director, John A. Ryan Institute;
Chair, Alan W. Moss Endowed Chair for Catholic Social Thought;
Professor of Catholic Studies and Ethics & Business Law
University of St. Thomas, Minnesota

"This is a wonderful and rare book. It communicates beautifully the truth of the depth of the person, the 'weight of glory' each person carries. It should be essential reading for all involved in catechesis. The chapters carefully unfold how we can better serve each precious soul, assisting each person to find his or her unique worth and calling within the glorious metanarrative of our heavenly Father's redemptive 'plan of the mystery' in Christ."

PETROC WILLEY
Professor of Catechetics, Franciscan University of Steubenville

"*Unrepeatable* is a call to all of us, personally and as a Church, to become more serious about vocations. The authors challenge each person to discover their call from God and to live it fully. St. John Paul II would be proud!"

ANDREAS WIDMER
Entrepreneur and author of *The Pope and the CEO*

"With *Unrepeatable,* authors Luke Burgis and Joshua Miller invite us into the cherished but often daunting role of helping those in our care to discover and embrace their own unique vocational callings. By delving beyond programs and policies into a unique appreciation of and respect for one another's stories, we learn not only the gifts we have to give, but also the ineffable bond which unites our common purpose. Pick up this book to help others, but be prepared to rediscover the blessing of your own story, too!"

LISA M. HENDEY
Author of *The Grace of Yes*

"Understanding and promoting personal vocations is one of the most important ways to unlock the potential for true human flourishing in our society. *Unrepeatable* is a timely book that outlines a unique process to discover personal vocation based on the wisdom of the Church and encourages all of us to embark on this game-changing journey."

BOB KEITH
Co-Founder, The Ciocca Center for Principled Entrepreneurship

"Little by little the realization is sinking in among serious Christians that everyone has a vocation—the unique calling that each of us receives from God to play a unique and unrepeatable part in God's redemptive plan. *Unrepeatable* will do much good by hastening the spread of a hugely important insight among an ever growing number of people. This book by Luke Burgis and Joshua Miller is clear, practical, and very much to the point. I recommend it highly."

RUSSELL SHAW
Author, *Personal Vocation: God Calls Everyone by Name, Catholic Laity in the Mission of the Church,* and other works

"*Unrepeatable* is an essential guide for those who seek to discern God's calling in their lives and to discern how best to call forth God's calling in others, especially young people searching to find their place in God's intentions. We can best live out our callings when we first discern God's unrepeatable creation that is the beauty of each our lives, and then turn toward others and help them discover their amazing unique place in God's plans and ways."

KATHLEEN A. CAHALAN

Professor of Practical Theology, Saint John's University School of Theology and Seminary and author of *The Stories We Live: Finding God's Callings All Around Us*

"Joshua Miller and Luke Burgis get to the core of how to help young people find their way toward adulthood in a complex and changing culture. Filled with deep insight and practical direction, *Unrepeatable* will guide those working with younger generations to mentor powerfully."

MARK MATLOCK

President of Wisdom Works and author of several books including *Freshman: The College Student's Guide to Developing Wisdom*

"When Josh Miller was my student he wrote outstanding papers on the unrepeatability of each human person. In this book he is making an important practical application of what he learned: he is showing how each person can come to discern his or her unrepeatable calling in life. Miller is taking personalist philosophy out of the classroom and making it fruitful for young people looking for the meaning of their lives. He and Burgis have something life-giving to say to them."

JOHN CROSBY, PHD

Professor of Philosophy, Franciscan University of Steubenville

"There are few conversations more important than those involving a person's vocation. Sadly, these conversations are rare, even among the faithful for whom such conversations should be most natural and frequent. Burgis and Miller's *Unrepeatable* is rich with vocation stories and thoughtful cultural analyses that readers will be eager to engage with others. I highly recommend it to anyone seeking to facilitate more frequent and better conversations about life's purpose and our mission at this extraordinary moment."

TIM CLYDESDALE
Author of *The Purposeful Graduate: Why Colleges Must Talk to Students about Vocation*

Unrepeatable

Unrepeatable

CULTIVATING THE UNIQUE
CALLING OF EVERY PERSON

Luke Burgis & Joshua Miller, PhD

EMMAUS
ROAD
PUBLISHING

www.EmmausRoad.org
Steubenville, Ohio

Emmaus Road Publishing
1468 Parkview Circle
Steubenville, Ohio 43952

Library of Congress Cataloging-in-Publication Data
Names: Burgis, Luke, author.
Title: Unrepeatable : cultivating the unique calling of every person / Luke
    Burgis and Joshua Miller.
Description: Steubenville : Emmaus Road, 2018.
Identifiers: LCCN 2017061868 (print) | LCCN 2018001558 (ebook) | ISBN
    9781947792692 (ebook) | ISBN 9781947792678 (hard cover) | ISBN
    9781947792685 (paper back)
Subjects: LCSH: Vocation--Christianity. | Storytelling--Religious
    aspects--Christianity. | Christianity and culture.
Classification: LCC BV4740 (ebook) | LCC BV4740 .B86 2018 (print) | DDC
    248.4--dc23
LC record available at https://lccn.loc.gov/2017061868

Cover image: ©charobnica / shutterstock.com

Cover design and layout by Margaret Ryland

To my father, Lee Rogers Burgis, and my mother, Ida Pauline Burgis, who have known my story and loved me from the beginning.

—LUKE—

To my parents, Arthur Franklin Miller III & Carol Koernig Miller, who so generously cultivated and continue to support my own unique calling.

—JOSHUA—

" . . . for Christ plays in ten thousand places,
Lovely in limbs, and lovely in eyes not his
To the Father through the features of men's faces."

—GERARD MANLEY HOPKINS—

Table of Contents

FOREWORD

GROWING UP has never been easy, and some would describe it as a lifelong process. But whether we define "growing up" as something that only ends when we die, or whether we think of it as those years of adolescence and young adulthood when a character is formed and a life path is embarked upon, growing up has become a lot harder because of the cultural tsunami that has swept through the Western world over the past fifty years or so.

That tsunami can be described in many ways, but the "Culture of Me" sums things up rather well. What the late Fr. Richard John Neuhaus used to call the "imperial autonomous Self" is at the center of the Culture of Me, and that Self has been cut off from some ideas that, for millennia, shaped the civilization of the West: like the idea that life is journey and pilgrimage, not cyclical repetition or one-thing-after-another; and the idea that there are truths written into the world and into us that we can know with clarity; and the idea that knowing those truths teaches us important things about ourselves and our obligations; and the idea that living according to those truths makes for happiness, fulfillment, and nobility; and the idea that if "Me" and my pleasures are all that I cherish, I've reduced myself to the condition of a two-year-old, no matter what my age.

Unrepeatable takes growing up far more seriously than the Culture of Me: indeed, Luke Burgis and Joshua Miller say to that culture, "We'll see you and raise you." We'll take the uniqueness of each individual person even more seriously than you do, Culture of Me. And we'll show you, from experience and from reflection, that taking the individual seriously means understanding that each of us grows up, or doesn't, because we grow out of the sandbox of self-absorption and enter a brighter, wider, more open and exciting world of vocation and mission—a world of wonder in which the driving question is, "What *ought* I be doing now?"

Which is a far cry from "What itch am I scratching now?"

There is an awful lot of unhappiness in the world of liberty-as-license, which is the great moral confusion within the Culture of Me, and there is some hope that young people are beginning to figure that out. Through stories, through the truths we learn from both revelation and reason, and through tales drawn from the experience of mentoring young people, *Unrepeatable* should help all those charged with helping the young grow up do that work well, especially those to whom young men and women turn with the burning question, "What am I supposed to do with my life?"

That question has as many answers as there are human beings, for each of us is indeed "fearfully and wonderfully made" (Ps 139:14). And here is another way that Luke Burgis and Joshua Miller offer a powerful antidote to one of the most disturbing, most degrading, aspects of the Culture of Me. Think of the vision of the human that emerges from the

New Atheists: the universe we know is a cosmic accident; we, and everything around us, are merely the byproducts of a chance convergence of cosmic biochemical processes; we're just congealed stardust, and when we die, we return to the meaningless oblivion from which we came.

Now if that's how you think of yourself, why not put the pleasure principle at the center of your life? If that's all there is, why leave the sandbox of self-infatuation? If that's all there can be, why sacrifice for someone else? In an easy-to-grasp way that is nevertheless rooted on some very deep thought, *Unrepeatable* offers an alternative to this degrading vision of human nature and human possibility, and thus fleshes out, for our confused cultural moment, what it means to grow into the "more excellent way" that St. Paul proposed to those cantankerous Corinthians, two millennia ago.

As his biographer, I'm frequently asked why St. John Paul II was such a magnetic Pied Piper for the young. My constant answer is that he was a compelling figure because he told the truth and he challenged the young to live in the truth. He didn't hedge, and he didn't pander. He knew that all of us fail, but he also knew that failure is no reason for young people to lower the bar of expectation or to lower their standards. Above all, he knew from his own experience as a university chaplain that young people want to lead lives of heroism, lives that count. So do Luke Burgis and Joshua Miller, and that knowledge permeates and informs this book.

Civilization itself depends on a critical mass of men and women who live vocationally—who live for others because they live according to the call to nobility and excellence that resonates in every human heart. *Unrepeatable* helps chart a path toward a better future than that proposed by the Culture of Me, and does so one life at a time.

—GEORGE WEIGEL
Distinguished Senior Fellow and William E. Simon Chair in Catholic Studies, Ethics and Public Policy Center

ACKNOWLEDGMENTS

Luke Burgis

THIS BOOK is the fruit of many years spent wrestling with God over my own personal vocation. My parents, Lee and Ida Burgis, my grandmother, Verna Bartnick, and my godmother, Mary Kelly, planted the seed of faith. Many others watered it.

I could not have made the journey without the constant and unwavering support of the Most Reverend Joseph A. Pepe, Bishop of Las Vegas, Fr. John Assalone, Fr. Paul Donlan, Fr. Brendan Hurley, and Rick and Tami Gordon. Their mentorship has been for me a model for building a culture of vocation.

Thank you to my friend and partner, Dr. Joshua Miller, whose loving attentiveness has helped me and so many others understand their God-given design. His life's work is what made this book possible, and his encouragement allowed me to be a part of it.

Special thanks go to Claire Alsup. My writing would be a shadow of itself without her surgical editing and zero-tolerance policy for cheesiness (what's left is my own). She also kept me well fed. Without that, no decent writing would have happened.

Thank you to all of my friends who have engaged me in spirited dialogue about the topics in this book and helped me to clarify my thoughts, especially David Jack, John Souder, Luke Brown, and Justin Conover.

Pope St. John Paul II, under whose patronage we have placed our work on personal vocation and whose example and teaching we have drawn on for so much of this book, is the inspiration behind the title "Unrepeatable"—a word which he repeated often!

Joshua Miller

MY SPOUSE, Brooke, helped in countless ways to carry the load of family responsibilities during long days while I wrote. Far beyond that good gift is the blessing of her motherhood to each of our children: David, Virginia, Nancy, Christopher, Joseph, Martin, and Evelyn Rose. Thank you, lovely wife!

I am grateful also to our children, each a dynamic and unrepeatable image bearer of Christ. It is an awesome privilege to help cultivate their own unique callings and I have learned much through the challenge and joy of that holy task.

My parents, Arthur and Carol Miller, to whom I dedicate this book, are unflagging in their generous support of my family and me. In a special way I thank my father, who over many years taught me the craft of story-based motivational patterning.

During the writing of this book my grandfather, Arthur Franklin Miller, Jr. passed away at the age of ninety-four. His pioneering work of discovering the phenomena of innate motivational patterns within achievement stories and his decades-long quest to champion that truth is a legacy for which I will be eternally grateful. *Requiscat in pace.*

The poet Nancy Anne Miller, my grandfather's widow, always enriches me with fine conversation, especially about human giftedness—and especially over Anchor Steam beer! I pray God for many more years of such discussion.

My co-author and friend, Luke Burgis, is a force of nature. Without his energy, intelligence, and drive I would still be plodding along in rough draft mode. I am deeply grateful for his partnership. The best of this book is his work.

Five years ago I began a journey to develop MCORE (Motivational Core), an automated assessment of unique motivational design based on the System for Identifying Motivated Abilities (SIMA®), with a group of colleagues from various disciplines: Tony Kroening, Rod Penner, Randy Zimmerman, Peter Larson, and Todd Hall, as well as my father, Arthur Miller III. They always believed that MCORE could be a critical part of helping young people discern their callings. They were right. Thank you gentlemen!

For nearly twenty years I have had the privilege of working with and serving many fine persons in SIMA® International, the company founded by my grandfather in 1961. Each of these folks has enabled me to grow in an understanding of human persons and how to help them flourish. I thank Rob and Mark Stevenson, Steven Darter, Suz Grimes, Don Kiehl, Kim Miller, Nick Isbister, Jude Elliman, Tommy

Thomas, Laura Coverstone, Bill Hendricks, Nancy Moore, Ed Poff, and Ron Evans.

David Schmiesing gave me the first opportunity to build curriculum around personal vocation that draws on MCORE when he asked me to help develop the Center for Leadership at Franciscan University of Steubenville. Many thanks to David as well as to our colleague at the Center, Ron McNamara, a rock of support.

Final acknowledgement goes to Dr. John Crosby, who taught me philosophy of the human person at Franciscan University of Steubenville and helped me understand both the distinctiveness of my grandfather's work and how it could be enriched through the Christian philosophical tradition.

INTRODUCTION

Luke Burgis and Joshua Miller

You lose yourself, you reappear
You suddenly find you got nothing to fear
Alone you stand with nobody near
When a trembling distant voice, unclear
Startles your sleeping ears to hear
That somebody thinks they really found you

—BOB DYLAN—

"It's Alright, Ma (I'm Only Bleeding)"

IT WAS May 17, 1966. Bob Dylan was playing to a crowd of about two thousand at the Free Trade Hall in Manchester, England. With his acoustic guitar slung over his shoulder and a wooden harmonica strapped to his neck, he warble-crooned his way through tracks from his new album, *Blonde on Blonde*, released the day before. In "Visions of Joanna," he sang the words "the ghost of electricity howls in the bones of her face." It was an ominous line.

On this world tour, Dylan had been shaking up fans by switching to an electric guitar for his second set, a

1

shocking departure from his folk music roots. The fans in Manchester heard the news, but many of them didn't want to believe it.

Dylan closed his first set with "Mr. Tambourine Man," bowed, and walked off the stage. The audience was edgy.

After the intermission, Dylan strutted back out. He had his band, the Hawks, with him, and a '65 black Fender Stratocaster electric guitar with a maple cap neck slung on his shoulder. Bassist Rick Danko plugged a Fender Jazz Bass into an amplifier.

Guitarist Robbie Robinson smashed into a riff for "Tell Me, Momma." The sound system in the hall wasn't made for the raw, visceral power of the music. Fan C.P. Lee said it "felt like I was being forced back in my seat, like being in a jet when it takes off." Dylan raised the volume of his voice to match the intensity of his band.

Between songs, he paced the stage in silence, tuning his guitar and mumbling in a raspy voice. Caterwauls of protest broke out in the audience. Fans started squabbling. Dylan charged forward, playing song after song of high-decibel rock: "Just Like Tom Thumb's Blues," "Leopard-Skin Pill-Box Hat," "One Too Many Mornings." With each song, Dylan grew more emboldened. So did his fans. The music was loud, mercurial, and violent.

After "Ballad of a Thin Man," the penultimate song of the night, there was a nervous quiet in the smoke-filled hall. Emotional exhaustion. It felt like the air had been sucked out of the place.

Then a disillusioned fan on the second floor balcony cried out, "Judas!" Everyone in the hall heard it, including

Dylan. On bootleg recordings of the concert available today, the heckler's voice still pierces the silence.

In the history of heckling, the "Judas" barb stands apart. It's the accusation that one is a traitor, not true to oneself, and not true to one's friends—or fans. The only thing worse is the rebuke of Peter: to be called "Satan." Neither is good.

Dylan strummed his guitar and responded, "I don't believe you." He started plucking the strings of his Fender. "You're a liar!" he added. Then Dylan turned his back to the crowd, instructed his band to play loud (using much more colorful language), and blew everyone away with a booming version of "Like a Rolling Stone." When he sang, "How does it feel?" it sounded like an accusation, not a question. His whole body writhed, and he poured his voice into his microphone like he wanted it to climb down his heckler's throat.

THE STORY OF STORIES

When Bob Dylan heard a voice call him "Judas," he knew it wasn't the voice of someone who truly knew him. It wasn't the voice of the one who called him from the beginning. Dylan recognized the lie because he knew his own story.

Dylan is a master storyteller. He won the Nobel Prize in Literature in 2016 for "having created new poetic expressions within the great American song tradition."[1] Before he told stories, he listened to stories—especially both the story of salvation and the story of his life. Because he did

---

[1] "Nobel Prize in Literature 2016, Bob Dylan," https://www.nobelprize.org/nobel_prizes/literature/laureates/2016/dylan-facts.html.

this, he understood his personal evolution even when others could not.

Dylan listened to our human story, which is caught up in a divine comedy of creation, rebellion, redemption, and restoration. He didn't learn about it as a third-person observer, but as someone caught up in the drama. Living the story allowed him to make sense of his life and the events unfolding in the world when he was coming of age (the Cold War, the Space Race, the Civil Rights Movement) because he knew the plot.

Dylan's writing reveals the extent to which he assimilated the Christian narrative into his life. In his early years in Greenwich Village, the American Civil War fascinated him. But he didn't see it merely as the bloody, mindless death of seven hundred fifty thousand people. "Back there, America was put on the cross, died, and was resurrected," he wrote in his memoir. "There was nothing synthetic about it. The godawful truth of that would be the all-encompassing template behind everything that I would write."[2]

He didn't learn the godawful truth about human nature from the Civil War. He learned it from Sacred Scripture and the history of the Church. He saw life, death, and resurrection happening all around him. He took his culture seriously, and he knew where it came from.

God breaks into lives and changes trajectories in a heartbeat. He never destroys history, though. He redeems it.

Dylan knew that his musical evolution was authentic

---

[2] Bob Dylan, *Chronicles* (New York: Simon & Schuster Paperbacks, 2005), 86.

because he knew what was driving it. He didn't adopt a "hermeneutic of discontinuity," which does away with the past. Pope Benedict XVI spoke frequently about the dangers of this disconnected hermeneutic, or way of interpretation, when speaking about the Church's liturgy. A hermeneutic of "reform," he wrote, must be seen within a hermeneutic of continuity.[3] This was Dylan's approach. He saw his life unfolding as one continuous story. He understood his evolution as an artist through the whole of his life.

According to the French philosopher Jean-François Lyotard, the mark of postmodernism is "incredulity toward metanarratives," or a refusal to accept the story that we're all immersed in—like a leaf that doesn't accept the tree it's growing on. Dylan, the most modern of men, didn't adopt this incredulity. He rooted himself in our human story and the personal stories of the people around him, stories bound together by timeless truths. Because he did this, he was able to make some of the most powerful music of the twentieth century.

This book is about how we can know and love others authentically by entering into their stories and paying attention to their unique, unrepeatable essence, which bears the fingerprints of God. We focus on how parents, coaches, educators, and other adult leaders ("mentors") can better cultivate the vocations of the young people in their care ("mentees"). When a mentee is deeply known and loved, he

---

[3] Pope Benedict XVI, Address to the Roman Curia Offering Them His Christmas Greetings (December 22, 2005), available from http://w2.vatican.va/content/benedict-xvi/en/speeches/2005/december/documents/hf_ben_xvi_spe_20051222_roman-curia.html.

is like a plant that bends toward the sun and blossoms in its rays. In the light of that loving relationship, he is free to discover, embrace, and fully live out his personal calling.

The life of each person can't be understood in a snapshot, a resume, or a social media profile. We have to enter fully into the stories of each individual if we hope to know and love them as God does. He is the *archégos*—the Author—of every human life (Acts 3:15).

And God is an author worth reading.

LISTENING TO LIVES

Bob Dylan made powerful music because he was tuned into the great symphony of life.

Every life is a song. In order to hear it, we have to enter into its rhythm and listen closely for the bass line and melody. The shape of God's design—what Gerard Manley Hopkins calls a thing's *inscape*—isn't revealed in one note. It's revealed in the fugue, the pattern of notes that play over and over in a person's soul. We hear it in their stories.

Stories give depth, texture, and meaning to the lives of the people we meet. They transform my neighbor in Apartment 2B from an abstraction into a flesh-and-blood person who was conceived at an exact time, whose mom ate pickle and peanut butter sandwiches during her pregnancy, who was raised in Faith, South Dakota, and who loves to eat Mini Babybel cheese wheels in her apartment while watching reruns of *Seinfeld*. Her name is Kate.

But those are just facts. They give me a glimpse of Kate from the outside, but they don't allow me to see her from the inside—her unique nature. In order for that image to emerge, we need to go deeper.

What happens when I ask Kate to tell me about a time in her life when she did something well and found it deeply satisfying? She grins and rocks excitedly in her chair. "Well . . . it might not sound like a big deal, but I canned tomatoes for the first time last year and made a homemade pasta sauce with them for my family at Christmas. Everyone loved it!"

This is what we call an *Achievement Story*. It's a particular kind of story that provides rich insight into a person's essence. When people tell these kinds of stories, they struggle for words. They're trying to describe an unrepeatable, ineffable experience that is uniquely their own.

Résumé questions excite no one. You've heard them all before: What were your responsibilities at your last job? What are your top three strengths? How well do you work in a team? They don't cut to the heart of the person. Anyone who goes on more than a few interviews can rattle off answers to these questions with robotic precision.

But "eulogy" questions—the questions that people ask about someone who dies—are much harder to answer. What did they love to do? What were they most proud of? Where did they find fulfillment? In the twilight of life, these are the questions that really matter. But we should ask them before the twilight.

Listening to Achievement Stories helps us to break through stereotypes. It reveals a person in her uniqueness and unrepeatability. This uniqueness is not only rooted in how she was created (for instance, her DNA) but in the freely chosen actions that have shaped her life. Her self-creative actions, especially when they bring joy, bear the fingerprints of God. They help reveal what psychologist James Hillman called "the soul's code," the unique design of the soul that is analogous to the uniqueness of one's body.

We all desire to be deeply known. But how many people who know you could tell the story of one of your most deeply joyful achievements? If you're like most people, you've never even been asked to share that story.

Our children deserve better. They know what we've forgotten: God created each of them with a unique, unrepeatable design, and He saw that it was good. It's up to us to help them discover, embrace, and live it to the full so that they may achieve the end for which they were made.

We can do that by listening attentively, asking good questions, and entering into their stories with the intent to see its unique form, the pattern of God's design.

In the following chapters, we'll share our combined twenty-five years of experience using a story-driven process that helps parents, teachers, coaches, and pastors enter deeply into the lives of others in order to help them discover their created design—and ultimately their vocation. In order to create a "culture of vocation," we have to create a culture of encounter—of truly *knowing* one another.

THE WAY OF EACH PERSON

In his poem "The Road Not Taken," Robert Frost writes, "Two roads diverged in a wood, and I— / I took the one less traveled by, / And that has made all the difference."

In today's world, there are thousands of voices telling

us which road to take. Every week there's a new voice pro-claiming the "way" forward—a new program, two roads, three keys, five forgotten principles, or seven *somethings*. If we could just follow the right path, it would make all the difference.

But our journey is more epic than that. It's not a walk in the woods. It's *The Odyssey*.

The ways that we have to travel are broader, longer, higher, and deeper than we can imagine. According to St. John Paul II, there are 7,484,325,476 of them—that's the total number of people in the world at the time of this writing.[4]

The pope wrote in his first encyclical that each human person is the "primary and fundamental way for the Church"[5] The way forward is not about following programs and methods. The way is persons.

We can't know the truth about someone without knowing his story. Truth has a story because the Truth is a person, Jesus of Nazareth—and every person has a story. If we are to know the truth about any person, we have to know his story. "What is in question here," wrote John Paul II, "is man in all his truth, in his full magnitude. We are not dealing with the abstract man, but the real, concrete, historical man" (RH 13).

We don't unite ourselves to Christ in an abstract way. The union happens in the real, concrete, historical cir-cumstances of life: care for the crying baby in the crib, the

---

4   United States Census Bureau, 2016. If we include the unborn (approx-imately 200 million), the total is closer to 7,684,325,476.

5   Pope John Paul II, On the Redeemer of Man *Redemptor Hominis* (March 4, 1979), no. 14, available from http://www.vatican.va (hereaf-ter cited in text as RH).

inconvenient phone call from a friend, and the sacrifice of the beer undrunk because we had to write a legal brief by the morning.

The nature of the union changes with the seasons of life. A man suffering from a debilitating disease is united to Christ on the Cross. On the day of his wedding, he was united to Christ at Cana in the celebration and joy of the feast.

Redemption is also not an abstract affair. Redemption for a mother who has lost her child is not a general redemption. It is being able to hold her child once again in the kingdom of heaven. Her entire *self* is redeemed, with all of her history.

Thomas Merton writes about this in his book *New Seeds of Contemplation*:

> The object of salvation is that which is unique, irreplaceable, incommunicable—that which is myself alone. This true inner self must be drawn up like a jewel from the bottom of the sea, rescued from confusion, from indistinction, from immersion in the common, the nondescript, the trivial, the sordid, the evanescent.[6]

How can we walk the way of each person when there are seven-and-a-half billion people on the planet? On our own, we can't. We can only do it as a Church. Because we

---

[6] Thomas Merton, *New Seeds of Contemplation* (New York: New Directions Publishing, 2007), 38.

are one Body in Christ, an encounter with one person is an encounter with Christ, through whom all things were created. The love of Christ has 7,484,325,476 unrepeatable ways of expression on the earth at this moment.

Each way ends in the mystery of God.

UNREPEATABLE LOVE

Every vocation is a call to love in a unique and unrepeatable way. Cultivating the vocation of a person, then, is about helping her to fully and authentically embrace the way that she is called to love—her personal way of receiving and giving love, of uniting herself with Christ, and of surrendering herself to grace. In becoming who she is, she becomes capable of loving God and neighbor with every fiber of her being.

Cultivating vocations requires a profoundly patient, kind, and gentle love like the love of Christ that St. Paul speaks about it in his First Letter to the Corinthians.[7] It's easy to hand a man a Bible; it's hard to enter into his life and accompany him. Sometimes, instructing a person in the faith can be about our own fulfillment. But standing with him in the gap as he grapples with the realities of faith in Jesus Christ involves sacrifice, including letting go of our own ideas about who he is and surrendering to God's.

---

[7] 1 Corinthians 13:4–7: "Love is patient and kind; love is not jealous or boastful; it is not arrogant or rude. Love does not insist on its own way; it is not irritable or resentful; it does not rejoice at wrong, but rejoices in the right. Love bears all things, believes all things, hopes all things, endures all things."

In Fyodor Dostoevsky's book, *The Brothers Karamazov*, Fyodor Karamazov observes, "The more I love humanity in general the less I love man in particular. . . . It has always happened that the more I hate men individually the more I love humanity." Fyodor is driven solely by his own fulfillment. He can scarcely imagine that he has some role to play in the fulfillment of others.

Jesus takes a radically different approach. In the Gospel of John, a Samaritan woman goes to an ancient well to draw water. She arrives to find Jesus sitting beside the well, "wearied as he was with his journey" (John 4:6). He's thirsty. In His humanity, He's thirsty for water. In His divinity, He thirsts for her life.

Jesus asks the Samaritan woman to give Him a drink, which confuses her. How can He, a Jew, be asking a Samaritan woman for a drink? Jews didn't associate with Samaritans. Jesus then shifts the conversation away from His thirst to hers. He tells the woman that it's she who should be asking Him for a drink of water. "Every one who drinks of this water will thirst again, but whoever drinks of the water that I shall give him will never thirst" (John 4:13–14).

"Sir, give me this water, that I may not thirst, nor come here to draw" (John 4:15), she says. The Samaritan woman was caught in a cycle of use and abuse. This is why she had to keep coming back to the well to fill up her bucket. The bucket is her dependence. No matter how many times she went to the well, she would never be satisfied. We learn this when Jesus reveals that he knows her story: "[Y]ou have had five husbands, and he whom you now have is not your husband" (John 4:18).

We don't know what else happened at the well that afternoon. We can imagine that Jesus, as He did to so many others, looked at her lovingly. He encountered her where she was. He entered into her life with the divine empathy that characterized his entire mission.

And then John tells us what happened to this woman: she left her bucket behind and went into the town to tell everyone about Jesus.

The woman came to the well seeking fulfillment that wouldn't last. She left with a vocation.

The Lord is our model. He shows us that sometimes we have to give people what they think they want in order to earn the right to give them what we know they need. The type of passionate love that seeks self-fulfillment—what the Greeks called *eros*—shouldn't end at *eros*. It's our job to cultivate it and transform it into the kind of love that seeks to fulfill others, what the New Testament calls *agape*. This is the distinctively Christian form of love. The foundation of both of these forms of love is fulfillment. In the one case, it's fulfilling *self*. In the other case, it's fulfilling *others*. In authentic love, they co-exist. Together, they allow the lovers' joy to be complete.

Young people stand before us with buckets in hand, waiting for someone to enter into their lives and awaken the kind of joy that makes them leave their buckets behind. C. S. Lewis summed up our responsibility in his sermon, *The Weight of Glory*: "The load, or weight, or burden of my neighbor's glory should be laid on my back, a load so heavy that only humility can carry it."[8] Our work is sacred because the weight we must carry is not a bucket, but glory. In the ancient Jewish mind, glory is something solid, concrete, and heavy. The weather isn't glorious. A rock is. And God's glory is the heaviest thing of all.

This book is about our neighbor's glory—his unique and unrepeatable way of glorifying God. It's our responsibility as Christians to put his glory on our backs, helping him to discover, embrace, and live his unique, personal calling so that he may hear and respond to the singular Word, the *Logos*, that spoke him into existence.

---

[8] C. S. Lewis, *The Weight of Glory* (New York: HarperCollins, 2001), 45.

1

KNOWING OUR CULTURE

Luke Burgis

"The Gospel lives always in conversation with culture,
for the Eternal Word never ceases to be present to
the Church and to humanity. If the Church holds
back from culture, the Gospel itself falls silent."

—POPE JOHN PAUL II—

DAVID FOSTER WALLACE told the story of two young fish who are swimming along when they pass an older fish swimming the other way. The old fish nods at them and says, "Morning, boys, how's the water?" The two young fish swim on for a while until finally one of them looks over at the other and asks, "What the hell is water?"

The point of the story is that the most immediate, ubiquitous, and important realities are often the hardest to see. We're the young fish. Rather than ask "How's the water?" we want to start with a more basic question: "What's water?" In other words, what reality are we immersed in?

The southern writer Flannery O'Connor, a keen observer of culture, once said, "If you live today you breathe in nihilism. In or out of the Church, it's the gas you breathe." That was in the 1950s. What about today? What are we breathing (or drinking)?

When children want to know how to name something, they point to it. "What is this?" they ask. "This" is a demonstrative word. We use it when something is so close to us that we can hold it in our hands, point to it, or demonstrate its presence. It's a key word in the institution of the Eucharist ("*This* is my body") because it points to a present reality: the Body and Blood of Jesus.

It's far more difficult, though, when we're immersed *in* something. There's not a distinct object to point to. "This" pervades every aspect of our life, to the extent that we might not even think about it.

Look around. Stick your finger in the air. Point at the air you breathe, the information you consume, and the taste of life on your tongue. It's *this*.

This is our water.

LIQUID MODERNITY

"The culture of liquid modernity has no 'populace' to enlighten and ennoble; it does, however, have clients to seduce."

—ZYGMUNT BAUMAN—
Culture in Modern Liquid Times

We're living in an age of "liquid modernity" according to sociologist Zygmunt Bauman. Everything is fluid, from identity to truth. There's angst and uncertainty about the future. By midnight we could be out of a job, out of a relationship, or out of battery life on our smartphone. In this ocean of uncertainty, what can we cling to?

In his *Introduction to Christianity*,[1] Cardinal Joseph Ratzinger (later Pope Benedict XVI) likens our situation to that of the main character in the play "The Satin Slipper" by Paul Claudel. Pirates loot the ship of a worldly Jesuit missionary and tied him to the mast of his sunken ship. The play opens with the missionary floating on a small piece of wood over the raging waters of the ocean: "Fastened to the cross—with the cross fastened to nothing, drifting over the abyss," writes Ratzinger.

In liquid modernity, personal vocation is the cross that each person is fastened to. It's the way that each person puts down roots in eternity—uniting himself to the Cross of Christ, which is planted firmly in heaven.

Culture develops on solid ground where people can put down roots. (The word "culture" comes from the root *cultus*, which originally meant tending or cultivating soil. It can drown in too much water.)

Meanwhile, the waters rage. If we don't understand the currents, we risk getting caught in the riptide.

There are three very strong currents that make the work of cultivating vocations a challenge. They contribute to the crisis in vocations, but that's okay. The word "crisis" comes from a Greek word, *krinein*, which implies decision, judgment, and discernment—all foundational elements of vocation. So let's enter into crisis.

---

[1] Cardinal Joseph Ratzinger, *Introduction to Christianity* (San Francisco: Ignatius Press, 1990), 18–19.

First, we live in a *culture of calculation*. A liquid culture loves numbers. They flow freely and they can become whatever we want them to be. "There are three kinds of lies: lies, damned lies, and statistics," wrote Mark Twain. Yet our culture prides itself on objective decision making through statistics. It falls prey to the illusion of complete certainty.

A few years ago, the bachelor CEO of a billion-dollar company told me that he was considering getting married, but he had one problem: he was a calculator. He looked at me seriously, with a hint of sadness, and said: "If you can prove to me scientifically that I will be happier if I get married, then I will get married." He's still not married.

Second, we live in a *culture of disincarnation*. According to the philosopher Fabrice Hadjadj, it's the crisis of "fake wood." First, we make laminate, then plywood, then particle board, then plastic with imitation wood grain. Finally, we put it in a Liquid Crystal Display (LCD) screen on a MacBook Pro and have a beautiful forest as our desktop background. We're undergoing the Great Liquidation of everything solid: wood, flesh, relationships, families, and faith.

Third, we live in a *culture of conformity*. Water takes the shape of the container that holds it. Our liquid culture is like a giant ice cube tray that never gets cold. We shake it and the water sloshes around from compartment to compartment. Lacking solidity, people flow easily into new cities, ideologies, and identities.

Leo Tolstoy began his novel *Anna Karenina* with the line, "Happy families are all alike; every unhappy family is unhappy in its own way." Vocations are the opposite. All saints are happy in different ways: each one lives out his personal vocation by finding his unique happiness in God. All sinners are unhappy in the same way: they choose not to respond to the call of God and live without the only thing that could make them truly happy.

A CULTURE OF CALCULATION

"Life is not a problem to be solved,
but a mystery to be lived."

—GABRIEL MARCEL—

playwright and philosopher

On opening night of the 2002 baseball season, Oakland Athletics' fans had bacon fat dripping from their beards—they love their bacon-wrapped Colossal Dogs there—and confidence brimming over their beer cups. The A's had been on a baffling tear for the past three seasons. They made the playoffs each year and took the New York Yankees to the brink of elimination twice, even though the Yankees outspent them by $86 million. "Something strange [was] happening in Oakland," as one sportscaster put it.

Jeremy Giambi kicked off the game with a line drive single to left field off of Texas Rangers' pitcher Chan Ho Park. Perhaps not a wave-worthy hit, but Giambi did what the A's did best: he got on base. That year the A's touched first base another 2,132 times (a .339 on-base percentage) and went on a twenty-game winning streak, something no American League team had done in the history of baseball.

The eccentric general manager of the cash-strapped Oakland A's, Billy Beane, had spent the past three seasons crafting a team that found gritty ways to win. Shortly after taking over the job in 1997, he implemented an empirical approach to evaluating players. He hired statisticians to bracket out all the fluff (the beauty of a player's swing or his marketability) and evaluate players based purely on the numbers that win baseball games—things like weighted on-base average (wOBA) and batting average on balls in play (BABIP). The emphasis on statistics was so serious that Beane and his staff were suspicious of in-person interactions with new players for fear of being swayed by non-objective measures.

Though Beane used sabermetrics (very effectively), he did not develop or name this approach. But it was so successful that other teams eventually adopted the system, and it spawned the entire business of "sports analytics." In 2003, Michael Lewis wrote a best-selling book about the rise of sabermetrics called *Moneyball: The Art of Winning an Unfair Game*. The book was so popular that it was eventually made into a movie starring Brad Pitt as Billy Beane. Thus the term *moneyball* entered the general lexicon.

And that's how baseball, the romantic game of summer nights filled with peanuts and cracker jacks and cold beer, became a calculated affair.

For many people, life had already become one. "Playing the cards we're dealt" is part of the American consciousness. Books and blogs about "life hacking" (tips, tricks, and shortcuts to increase efficiency and happiness) are some of the most popular. Lewis' book was a success not only because he's a good storyteller, but because he told the same story that we were already living: "Life: The Art of Winning an Unfair Game."

The Poker Game of Discernment

God is not a Sadistic Poker Player. Yet this is the image that many young people unknowingly have of Him. He holds the cards of our lives in His hands. He knows the secret to our best life and true happiness, but He won't tell. We don't even know if He's holding a good hand or a bad hand. Worse yet, He might be bluffing.

Those who don't believe that they have a vocation (or that there is even a reality called vocation) still have to contend with Him. Their poker player simply deals in desire. Which desires lead to fulfillment, and which lead to emptiness? He'll never tell.

A human being has thousands of conflicting and competing desires nearly every day. Without grace and virtue, and especially without a clear idea of where he's going, he has no way to order them. Desires can deceive, and nobody is better at deception than a good poker player (especially a sadistic one). This mentality makes decision making tortuous—even when a choice is between good things.

When I go to a restaurant, I sometimes get menu anxiety. I don't want to order the steak if the place is known for its fish. And how do I know whether the "special" seafood salad is delicious or just a clever way to get rid of old fish? If you hand me a wine list, things get even more complicated. I don't like to make poor choices. How am I supposed to know whether the Lebanese Syrah is overpriced relative to Super Tuscan? After I choose, I want to hear the words, "Good choice."

If I have this much anxiety over mundane choices, how much more anxiety do I have over the cards that the Sadistic Poker Player is holding? My life is in his hands. I fear hearing the words "Wrong Choice" come from his cold, grey lips before he lays down his hand and laughs.

But Jesus doesn't greet people in heaven with "Good Choice." In the Parable of the Good Steward, the Master says, "Well done, good and faithful servant; you have been faithful over a little, I will set you over much; enter into the joy of your master" (Matt 25:21).

The Lord is not out to trick us. He is the Good Shepherd who desires our good, and He will lead us to that good if only we would follow Him. Indeed, He *is* the Good. This is why Jesus tells His servant to *enter into the joy of master.*

He tells the Samaritan woman at the well: "If you knew the gift of God" (John 4:10)! Vocation is a gift from God that brings joy to those who receive it.

Today recognizing the gift requires a new kind of openness.

The Gift That Opens

Some gifts are meant to be opened. Other gifts are meant to open us. How can we know the difference?

There's evidence that our Western culture may not easily grasp what is *given.* In his book, *The Master and His Emissary*, Iain McGilchrist shows that there has been an increasing reliance on the left hemisphere of the brain over the past few hundred years (a result of Cartesian dualism, the industrial revolution, technology, and other factors). As a consequence, we live a more calculated life, relating to the world in a way that is suspicious of gifts. Calculated living prefers earning, not receiving. It's the world of Moneyball and poker, not falling in love.

The right brain (the "Master") is an open system where we take in new experiences, seeing the whole rather than the parts. It's where we wonder. The left brain (the "Emissary") is different. It's a closed system that operates within the boundaries of what it has received. It likes "certainty" more than adventure, maps more than metaphor, mechanisms more than living things. New experiences are *re*-presented—the left brain takes data from the right brain and processes it. It fits experiences into categories, frameworks, and patterns.

The two hemispheres of the brain see the world in radically different ways, but they have a partnership. The right brain gives us a way of seeing the world that is open to the dynamism of new experiences and the left brain gives us a way to find meaning and structure in those experiences. As the right brain takes in new aspects of reality, the left brain constantly revises its models in order to make sense of what it is receiving. There's a feedback loop.

But what happens if the left brain becomes dominant? Then we live in a society where new, unexpected experiences can't be fully received and we're left trying to understand the world in bits and bytes of fragmented information without their full context. *Donum* (gift) becomes *data.*

The left brain is good at "calculating thought" and the right brain is good at "meditative thought."[2] Calculating

---

[2] The two modes of thinking described by the philosopher Martin Heidegger.

thought is always concerned with how to reach its objective. How can I win more games? How can I win this poker hand? It calculates options. It assigns values. It maximizes the chances of winning. Meditative thought is patient thought. It doesn't look immediately for solutions. It doesn't calculate options or project itself into the future. Instead, it remains in the present and sinks deeper into it, allowing reality to unfold. It asks questions like: What present is this? Why is it here? How did it get here? What does it hide? What does it reveal? What does it mean?

The right brain likes to *wonder* more than calculate. And it's only with this meditative habit of being that we can earnestly enter into another's story—even our own.

Wonder is the attitude that people have in the presence of Jesus in the Gospels. The Greeks called the object of this wonder *téras* (τέρας), which means "something beyond all expectation."

If people expected something from God in first-century Palestine, it certainly wasn't Jesus of Nazareth. The Incarnation of the Son of God didn't just surpass expectations—it shattered them. This is God's style.

Grace is the gift beyond all expectation. God eludes our best efforts to wrap our minds around Him and grace breaks into our lives in unexpected ways. In Flannery O'Connor's writing, grace is never a pious sentiment in a pew but something more like an unexpected punch in the face (sometimes literally).

The calculating mind simply can't experience anything beyond all expectation. It can only manipulate what it is has already received, putting it into a box (or "category") and calculating what to do next. But when we approach life with meditative thought (wonder), we find that each person—indeed, each thing—is truly beyond all expectation.

A CULTURE OF DISINCARNATION

"Have you entered the storehouses of the snow?"

—JOB 38:22—

Wilson Bentley was born in the winter of 1865 on a farm in Jericho, Vermont—the heart of the snowbelt—as the Civil War was drawing to a close. Nature captured his imagination from a young age. He studied spiderwebs, grasshoppers, caterpillars, and anything else he could get his hands on.

He loved to show his mother his new discoveries. He'd catch a butterfly and run home with the tiny creature tickling his palms. In the winter, Willie was obsessed with snow. What is it? What does it look like up close? Why does it melt so quickly? He caught snowflakes in his hands and on his tongue, but they always melted before he had a chance to study them.

Willie's mother Fanny was a former schoolteacher who noticed and nurtured his sense of wonder. On his fifteenth birthday, she gave him an old microscope that she had used in her classroom. Willie was ecstatic. He could finally study all of his small discoveries in depth—especially snowflakes.

Willie stood outside in sub-zero weather and caught snowflakes on a black tray. Then, he quickly placed them under his microscope. He tried to draw them, but he only had a few minutes to look at them before they melted, never long enough to capture the full design.

The beauty and complexity of each snow crystal was beyond anything that he ever expected to see. Each crystal had six branches that were exactly alike, but each crystal seemed to be completely different from every other crystal. Willie realized that he needed some way to capture the unique designs that he saw, or else his discoveries would be lost to the world forever.

When he was fifteen, Willie read about a new product from the Bausch and Lomb Optical Company that combined a microscope with a bellows camera. He thought that it might be the key to unlocking the mystery of the snowflake, but it cost almost one hundred dollars, which was an enormous sum of money in the late nineteenth century. For months, Willie begged his parents to buy it for him. His father balked. The instrument cost as much as his entire herd of cattle. How could he justify spending that much money to look at snowflakes?

His mother, knowing her son's genuine desire to share what he had seen, interceded on his behalf and prevailed in convincing her husband that it would be good for their son. Before the end of the year, Willie's parents made the sacrifices necessary to buy the equipment.

Even with his state-of-the-art equipment, snowflakes were elusive. On the coldest of days, Willie had only six or seven minutes to get a photograph before the snowflakes melted. Finally, after four years of repeated failures and modifications to his equipment, Willie had a breakthrough. On a stormy day in 1885, he developed his first negative photograph of a snowflake. He could share the "miracle of beauty" that had captivated him since his youth.

In the forty-six winters that remained in his life, Wilson Bentley photographed over five thousand snow crystals. It became his life's work. He invested over $15,000 but received less than $4,000 in compensation for his photographs. This didn't bother him. "The recognition has been very gratifying, but not very remunerative," he wrote. "I am a poor man, except in the satisfaction I get out of my work. In that respect I am one of the richest men in the world. I wouldn't trade places with Henry Ford or John D. Rockefeller for all their millions!"[3]

Wilson became one of the world's most recognized experts on snow, and a pioneer in the field of photomicrography, the photography of small objects. Throughout his life, he gave away hundreds of photographs as gifts and made slideshows of snowflakes for children in his neighborhood. Toward the end of his life, he gave most of his remaining photographs and study notes to universities and private foundations.

In November 1931, Wilson compiled twenty-five hundred of his best images in a book. In it, he wrote

Under the microscope, I found that snowflakes were miracles of beauty; and it seemed a shame that this beauty should not be seen and appreciated by others. Every crystal was a masterpiece of design and no one design was ever repeated. When a snowflake melted,

---

[3] Duncan C. Blanchard, *The Snowflake Man: A Biography of Wilson A. Bentley* (Granville, OH: McDonald and Woodward Publishing Company, 1998) 70.

that design was forever lost. Just that much beauty was gone, without leaving any record behind.[4]

A month after the book was published, Wilson walked six miles home during a snowstorm to the same farm where he was born, contracted pneumonia, and died two weeks later. He was buried at Jericho Center Cemetery under a small gravestone with three words on it: "Wilson: Snowflake Man."

Grasping Snowflakes

The wonder of Wilson Bentley's vocation is that he probably never thought about vocation at all, at least not theologically. He simply did what Annie Dillard describes in her essay "Living Like Weasels."

> We can live any way we want. People take vows of poverty, chastity, and obedience—even of silence— by choice. The thing is to stalk your calling in a certain skilled and supple way, to locate the most tender and live spot and plug into that pulse. This is yielding, not fighting. A weasel doesn't "attack" anything; a weasel lives as he's meant to, yielding at every moment to the perfect freedom of single necessity.[5]

---

[4] Blanchard, *The Snowflake Man*, 22.
[5] Annie Dillard, "*Living Like Weasels*," *Touchstone Anthology of Contemporary Creative Nonfiction: Work from 1970 to Present*, ed. Lex Williford and Michael Martone (New York: Simon & Schuster, 2007), 148–51.

Wilson located his most tender and live spot, grabbed hold of it, and never let go. He rarely left his small family farm in Jericho, but his life was charged with adventure. He discovered the grandeur of God in a snow crystal and he shared it with others.

Would Bentley have taken the time to contemplate a snowflake if he had been born today? We'll never know. Now students can plug into Google Maps and see the entire world with the click of a button. They can explore the structure of a snowflake from the comfort of an iPad. They don't have to submerge their ankles in snow until their toes go numb.

Philosopher Michael Polanyi wrote that it is not by looking at things but by *dwelling in them* that we understand their meaning. Wilson Bentley dwelt in the snow of the Vermont snowbelt for over sixty years—long enough for it to reveal its secrets. How long are we willing to dwell with the people we meet?

Learning from Nature

On a winter afternoon in 2017, I went to visit my co-author, Joshua, at his home in Toronto, Ohio, near the small university town of Steubenville. We paid a visit to his friends, Shawn and Beth Dougherty, who live on a family-scale sustainable farm in eastern Ohio.

The Dougherty's started the farm in 1996 on a piece of land that was deemed "unsuitable for agriculture" by the state of Ohio. They didn't know much about sustainable farming at the time, but they knew that they were the type of people who might enjoy watching bluebirds look for nesting holes in pasture fence posts or gloating over all the red, squirmy worms in a half-cooked pile of compost.

Shawn and Beth struck me with the colorful language that they use to describe things. Their desire to farm was not driven primarily by sustainability, veganism, or food sovereignty. It was about paying attention to grass, the texture of a calf coat, and the challenges of winter chicken culling. I didn't ask them, but I imagined that they would like Richard Wilbur's poem "Love Calls Us to the Things of This World" (the title speaks for itself).

An abstract, disincarnate world is full of limitless possibilities. But are more theoretical options always better? The population of bean beetles and cucumber bugs on the Dougherty's farm are *things*. They demand attention.

"When we give ourselves in commitment," Beth said, "it takes away the necessity of choosing between a more or less limitless set of possibilities. We find that we receive back things like time with our family and time spent marveling at the color of the summer wild flowers."

Shawn and Beth see the incarnate world, in all of its specificity and limitations, as the secret to cultivating a healthy sense of their own humanity. By choosing to raise their family while caring for a small piece of land in the hills of eastern Ohio, they are powerfully focused on a concrete mission that organizes their lives. "The power of a river is in its banks," Beth said. "If you take away its banks, it spreads out and becomes a lazy lake. But if you keep the banks firm—give the thing form—there's a lot of power behind it."

The first thing that I noticed when I visited Shawn and Beth's farm was their naturalness, which is a forgotten virtue in our technological age. Naturalness comes from nature—it can't be manufactured. There was no pretense (unlike an urban food startup that recently welcomed me with a PowerPoint presentation about their revolutionary "social" entrepreneurship in food agriculture). Beth greeted me with coffee.

Shawn and Beth work hard, and they love what they do. They're revolutionizing their piece of land.

In cultivating the soil, they are cultivating a way of life.

A CULTURE OF CONFORMITY

"The evil of our times consists in the
first place in a kind of degradation, indeed in a
pulverization, of the fundamental uniqueness
of each human person."

—KAROL WOJTYLA—
(St. John Paul II)
1968 Letter to Cardinal Henri de Lubac[6]

A 1985 commercial begins with a van pulling up to a beach on a sticky ninety-two-degree day. Loud speakers pop up from the roof. Inside the van, a bushy-haired, smiley-faced young man hops from the driver's seat into the back, which happens to be a fully outfitted recording studio. He pops the cap off a cold bottle of Pepsi a few inches away from a

---

[6] Michael Novak, foreword to *Karol Wojtyla: The Thought of the Man Who Became Pope John Paul II*, by Rocco Buttiglione, trans. Paolo Guietti and Francesca Murphy (Grand Rapids, MI: Eerdmans, 1997), xi.

microphone and the sound is amplified over the speakers.

Sunbathers hear gas bubbles popping, lusty gulps of soda, and a long, drawn-out, "Aahhhhh." Pure refreshment. Everyone on the beach rushes toward the van. Then the driver-turned-Pepsi-drinking-recording artist hops out, puts on a hat, and starts handing out bottles of ice-cold Pepsi to the parched crowd. The commercial closes with the slogan: "Pepsi: The Choice of a New Generation."

The irony is that the people on the beach don't appear to have any choice at all—and Pepsi knows it. The commercial is one of the first examples of advertising that is self-conscious. It makes fun of itself.

But there's a subtle trick. Brad, who works fifty-hour weeks as an entry-level accountant and took Marketing 101 as an undergraduate at Wake Forest University, watches the commercial from his couch and feels like he's in on the joke. He has transcended the "masses" that Pepsi targeted in the commercial. He's not like them. He has choices.

Then he goes to the store and buys more Pepsi.

Pepsi knows what every con man knows: the moment when people are most comfortable is the moment when they are most easily seduced. Just when Brad thinks he's free of manipulation, he's most open to the next cold beverage truck that pulls up. It might be full of Pepsi. Or it might be full of liberalism, socialism, populism, or some other thirst-quenching *ism*.

The French philosopher René Girard calls this a consequence of "mimetic desire," or the imitation of what others desire. It starts at a young age. At a birthday party, five-year-old Kelly grabs a balloon and shouts, "This balloon is mine!"

Suddenly, that balloon becomes the most coveted balloon in the room. Connor, playing with his big red truck, doesn't find it entertaining anymore because Kelly, with the perfect bows in her pigtails, loves her balloon so much.

When they grow older, the mimetic rivalry may not be over balloons, but it will endure. The mimetic mechanism is present in schools, restaurants, relationships, and every other domain of human life. According to Girard, it's also present deep within the human heart.

There's no escape from this condition. There's no option of non-conformity. The question is: To whom or to what will we conform our desires?

If we don't know, Pepsi does.

#ConformToMe

Our culture celebrates the free, autonomous self, yet we have a stultifying lack of differentiation. From the industrial-produced tomatoes on our tables to the cultural narratives that produce a chorus of politically correct phrases and opinions on college campuses, a homogenizing force is sweeping through our society. Our technocratic, mass-produced culture has resulted in an alarming degree of *sameness*.

When a person severs ties with the moral, cultural, and religious history that shapes our world, he trades the divine creativity for his own. He wants Hamlet without Shakespeare. He wants Bob Dylan without folk music.

In his short story "Unaccompanied Sonata," Orson Scott Card imagines a boy, Christian Haroldsen, who is a musical prodigy in a dystopian society run by authoritarians who control every aspect of society—including every person's vocation. At two years old, "his seventh battery of tests pinpointed the future he would inevitably follow." Christian would be a maker of music.

In order not to spoil his creativity, government authorities lock him in a cabin so that he can make truly original music. Christian is prohibited from listening to any other music that might corrupt his originality and make his music derivative.

One day, though, he secretly discovers Bach. And through Bach, he begins to discover himself.

When the Watchers (the authorities) find out that Christian's originality has been "corrupted," they forbid him from ever making music again. And so he tries to repress his irresistible, insatiable desire for musical expression.

Christian eventually takes a job as a deliverer of doughnuts to grocery stores. One evening after work, he wanders into Joe's Bar and finds a piano. At that moment, his desire to make music overwhelms all of the forces conspiring against him to stay silent. He sits down and plays the piano in a way that astonishes Joe, the bar owner. He played "as pianos aren't meant to be played; the bad notes, the out-of-tune notes were fit into the music so that they sounded right, and Chris's fingers, ignoring the strictures of the twelve-tone scale, played, it seemed to Joe, in the cracks."

He exercised his freedom in a culture of conformity. But soon after, he pays the consequences. The Watchers find him. One of them "took a laser knife from his coat pocket and cut off Christian's fingers and thumbs, right where they rooted into his hands." That's how a vocation dies.

Forces of Conformity

Who are the Watchers in our society? They don't cut off fingers and thumbs. They're far more subtle.

We can get an idea of how the Watchers—the forces of conformity—shape our world by looking at education, agriculture, technology, and language.

First, *education*. The American education system is a funnel, and students who want to excel in it are forced to conform if they want to come out the other end. Sir Ken Robinson, an expert on education (and author of the most watched TED talk of all time), says that "our education system has mined our minds in the way that we strip-mine the earth: for a particular commodity." The result has been a massive stunting of creativity. Many young people grow up striving to produce exactly the right type of résumé that will allow them to become productive members of society. They face batteries of standardized tests, interviews, and assessments to ensure the integrity of the commodities that our increasingly specialized world is looking for.

Second, *agriculture*. When man thinks that he is master over nature, even fruits and vegetables must conform. Biodiversity is decreasing rapidly. If a teenager saw the variety of Brandywine tomatoes in my mother's garden, he could be forgiven for thinking that something is wrong with them. Some of them look like monstrosities with their bumps and lumps and color variations. He's used to seeing large beefsteak tomatoes in supermarkets that are mass-produced on industrial farms in Florida and look like they came off of an assembly line. From the outside, they look like bright red ornaments that I could hang from my Christmas tree. And that's what they taste like. The Florida Tomato Committee has strict controls about which traits their tomatoes must possess: flawlessly smooth skin, evenly round shape, and consistent size. They're rejected if the shape and coloration don't conform to standards. And if biting into one of these uniform tomatoes doesn't produce mouth-watering satisfaction, that's okay—as long as they look like they should.

Third, *technology*. According to a new study by Common Sense Media, teens spend an average of nine hours every day using media. Evidence already suggests that smartphone usage is linked to skyrocketing rates of teen depression and suicide.[7] Today, the peers to whom they compare themselves and model behavior are not simply the twenty-five kids in their eighth grade classroom; they are the millions of teens bombarding them with Instagram, Twitter, and Facebook posts at all hours of the day and night. This has led to a widespread globalization of ideas, values, and structures that used to be formed in the home, school, and community.

Tech companies have tremendous power and influence. Amazon heavily shapes how people shop, Google how they acquire knowledge, and Facebook how they communicate. Twitter allows one million or more people to echo the exact words of another throughout the world within a matter of minutes. (In 2016, sixteen-year-old Carter Wilkerson authored the tweet with the most retweets in history: a request to win free chicken nuggets at Wendy's with the

---

[7] Jean M. Twenge, "Have Smartphones Destroyed a Generation?" *The Atlantic,* September 2017, https://www.theatlantic.com/magazine/archive/2017/09/has-the-smartphone-destroyed-a-generation/534198/.

tweet, "HELP ME PLEASE. A MAN NEEDS HIS NUGGS." It was retweeted over 3,650,000 times. By contrast, one of Pope Francis' most popular tweets, "Every Life is a gift. #marchforlife," was retweeted about 22,000 times.) It's easier than ever to "follow" people and ideas and propagate things we like—and it's a strange world where one man's quest for chicken nuggets is 165 times more interesting than the pope's words about the dignity of every human life.

Finally, *language.* The conformity of language, which shapes the way that we see the world, is a problem inside and outside of the Church. Inside the Church, we use terms like "vocation" in an equivocal way (we apply it to the calling of every person, and then exclusively to priests and religious in the next breath) and we can rattle off platitudes like Everything Happens for a Reason without taking the time to understand the person we're talking to. Outside of the Church, people are told what to do, what to eat, how to think, and how to speak. An Orwellian manipulation of language is becoming commonplace. (For instance, someone who disagrees with the government's new use of the word "marriage" is quickly labeled an ignorant bigot.)

Back in 1993, David Foster Wallace already noticed the dangerous way that mass media and advertising were shaping language. He bemoaned the state of fiction writing. Almost all of the popular new writers were mimicking the irony they saw on television. They were afraid to be serious. But in their quest for clever irony, writers were falling headlong into a cesspool of cheap marketing tactics. Wallace wrote, "The next literary 'rebels' in this country might well emerge as some weird bunch of anti-rebels . . . who treat of plain old untrendy human troubles and emotions in U.S. life with reverence and conviction."[8]

In a culture of conformity, we need more than rebels. A rebel becomes a reflection of the very culture that he sought to rebel against. Instead, we need men and women with a transcendent purpose to achieve—with a personal vocation. Saints aren't defined by what they are against, but by what they are for. They are anti-rebels par excellence.

The Anti-Rebel

In 1916, at the age of eighteen, Dorothy Day dropped out of the University of Illinois and moved to the Lower East Side of New York City. She abandoned her girlish interest in religion and fell in with a bohemian crowd that hung out in bars and coffee shops around Washington Square Park. She drifted naturally toward socialism. In her autobiography, she confessed to the temptation to solve everything with politics at that time in her life. "I wanted to go on picket lines, to go to jail, to write, to influence others and so make my mark on the world," she wrote.[9]

Dorothy spent most of her twenties "throwing herself down different avenues, looking for a vocation."[10] She took part in protests and marches, got arrested twice, and finally

---

[8] David Foster Wallace, "E Unibus Pluram: Television and U.S. Fiction," Review of Contemporary Fiction, 13:2 (1993: Summer), 192–193.

[9] Dorothy Day, *The Long Loneliness: The Autobiography of the Legendary Catholic Social Activist* (San Francisco: HarperOne, 1952), 60.

[10] David Brooks, *The Road to Character* (New York: Random House, 2015), 82.

found work as a journalist at the radical left-wing newspaper *The Call* for five dollars a week. Over the following years, she drifted aimlessly. At one point, she worked as a nurse at a Brooklyn hospital where she met Lionel Moise, a "womanizing newspaperman," and eventually became pregnant with his child. Moise told Dorothy to get an abortion, and she did.

Dorothy continued to fight for social justice and to write. Her novel *The Eleventh Virgin* was published and optioned for $5,000 by a Hollywood studio, but she eventually became so ashamed of it that she tried to buy up every copy. David L. Brooks, in his book *The Road to Character*, writes that, "Day was taking a stand against injustice, but she was doing it without an organizing transcendent framework. She seems to have felt, unconsciously and even then, that for her, activism without faith would fail."[11]

Dorothy began to realize that her activism and self-creative ambition—which was divorced from any living relationship with the infinitely creative God—was making her a worldly conformist. Instead of conforming to Jesus Christ, she was conforming herself to a political party, to an ideology, to the passing moment.

Dorothy sold the movie rights to *The Eleventh Virgin* and bought a beach house on Staten Island. She soon found a new lover, an anarchist and biologist named Forster Batterham who visited her at her bungalow on Staten Island almost every weekend for four years. Once again Dorothy became pregnant and this time gave birth to their baby girl, Tamar.

---

[11] Ibid., 81.

The birth of her daughter marked a profound change in Dorothy. She was overwhelmed with a sense of gratitude. "No human creature could receive or contain so vast a flood of love and joy as I often felt after the birth of my child. With this came the need to worship, to adore."[12] Dorothy began to pray again for the first time since she was a little girl. She stopped rebelling against worldly power and started rebelling against sin.

When it came time for her to find a spiritual home, she turned toward the Catholic Church. Her attraction to the Church didn't come from its political or social clout. "It was the people, not theology," writes Brooks. "It was the Catholic immigrants she had covered and served—their poverty, their dignity, their communal spirit, and their generosity toward those who were down and out."[13] Her contact with the poor was the most credible witness to the truths of the faith. Dorothy found the Church, and in it she found her vocation.

In 1938, she published an account of her conversion in a book titled *From Union Square to Rome*. In it she wrote that she would "try to trace for you the steps by which I came to accept the faith that I believe was always in my heart."[14] Dorothy stopped rebelling and started responding to the deepest desires of her heart—to the Word that was buried deep within it from the beginning.

---

[12] Day, *The Long Loneliness*, 135.
[13] *The Road to Character*, 85.
[14] Dorothy Day, *From Union Square to Rome* (Maryknoll, NY: Orbis Books, 2006), 3.

The *Catholic Worker* Movement that she founded is still thriving today with more than two hundred and forty communities in the U.S. and overseas committed to nonviolence, voluntary poverty, prayer, and hospitality for the homeless, exiled, hungry, and forsaken.

TOWARD A CULTURE OF VOCATION

A fresh and courageous perspective is needed to foster a culture of vocation. Because we live in a culture that is anti-vocational, a vocational culture is necessarily counter-cultural. It fosters meditative thought rather than calculating thought, prefers to touch a person rather than talk about an idea, and cultivates the freedom to imitate Christ rather than men.

We know that no vocation is possible without the grace of God. Yet grace is outside of our control, and talking about it too much can reduce it to something that we think we understand better than we do. We can't control God's grace, but we can dispose ourselves (and others) to it.

Fr. Herbert Alphonso, S.J., in his excellent book *Personal Vocation*, says that the spiritual exercises of St. Ignatius are about discerning one's personal vocation, which is founded on one's nature—"one's unrepeatably unique and specific way of actually *disposing* oneself for the Lord."[15] Fr. Alphonso humbly admits that God's grace is something outside of our

---

[15] Herbert Alphonso, *The Personal Vocation: Transformation in Depth Through the Spiritual Exercises* (Rome: Gregorian & Biblical Press, 2006), 92.

control, beyond all expectation. But we can and we must learn to dispose ourselves to it based on our unique nature.

We propose a simple approach: Listen to people's stories in order to help them discover their unique, motivational design. This gives them a hermeneutic, or interpretive key, to understanding their continued discernment. Then, in the light of faith, accompany them as they discover and embrace their unrepeatable call. Mentors have front seats to this unfolding of God's design. In the climactic meal of "Babette's Feast," General Lorens Löwenhielm—who, earlier in Isak Dinesen's short story, had become jaded by unrequited love and wrote the world off as cruel and unjust—is overcome with gratitude for God's mysterious design. He escaped a life of dealing with the Sadistic Poker Player.

During a meal with his old friends, including the woman who once spurned him, he becomes an instrument of grace for others. In the middle of the meal, after realizing that grace has broken into his life (and emboldened by a few glasses of Clos de Vougeot 1845), he stands up to make a toast:

> We have all of us been told that grace is to be found in the universe. But in our human foolishness and short-sightedness we imagine divine grace to be finite. For this reason we tremble. We tremble before making our choice in life, and after having made it again tremble in fear of having chosen wrong. But the moment comes when our eyes are opened, and we see and realize that grace is infinite. Grace, my friends, demands nothing from us but that we shall

await it with confidence and acknowledge it in gratitude.[16]

God's grace is an ocean, and we need only let ourselves get wet. To the question of the old fish, "How's the water today?" we can answer with confidence: Everywhere.

---

[16] Isak Dinesen, *Babette's Feast and Other Anecdotes of Destiny* (New York: Vintage Books, 1988), 40–41. See also the 1987 Danish film adaptation of *Babette's Feast*.

2

OUR UNIQUE MOTIVATIONAL DESIGN

The Seeds of Personal Vocation

Joshua Miller

"In God's plan, every man is born to seek self-fulfillment, for every human life is called to some task
by God. At birth a human being possesses certain
aptitudes and abilities in germinal form, and these
qualities are to be cultivated so that they may bear
fruit."

—BL. POPE PAUL VI—
On the Development of Peoples

S AM GARCIA hunkered down at Philip Morris head-
quarters to fill out yet another HR form.[1] He was asked
to complete the questionnaire as part of an executive development plan facilitated by Arthur Miller, Jr. of People

---

[1] This anecdote is based upon actual events. "Sam Garcia" is a
pseudonym.

Management Incorporated. Philip Morris had retained Miller to help the company make effective management decisions and Sam was the latest employee to go through the program.

The questions were simple but required him to reflect on his past. It was not an activity that Sam was used to.

Recall activities you deeply enjoyed doing and believe you did well. Go back as far as you can remember. Include activities from any sphere of life (church, family, professional, etc.). Describe what you did. What was satisfying about what you did?

And so, for a few hours, Sam recounted some apparently random activities beginning with a massive tree fort he had built in eighth grade and ending with a new database project he had recently finished at Philip Morris.

I have no idea what they'll get out of this, Sam thought. The exercise had been more interesting than he expected. Parts of his past buried by time had come, fondly, back to him. But *what does swinging a hammer have to do with software overhaul?* He submitted the form and went back to work.

Two weeks later Miller was given a Motivated Abilities Pattern® or MAP: a custom-tailored report describing a consistent structure of motivated behavior revealed in each of Sam's stories.

The MAP stunned Sam. It captured recurring ways he was most inclined to be and to act in the world, revealing a pattern of innate drives he had felt as early as he could remember but had not articulated. "How did you get that out of my stories?" he asked.

Miller described for Sam the beautiful phenomenon that when people describe activities they deeply enjoy doing and believe they do well, a recurring pattern of behavior, a structure of innate motivation, is manifested in their language.

"But, Art," Sam said, "I didn't write out a thematic document. There was no 'pattern' at all. I just jotted down a bunch of random memories." Then Sam asked the million-dollar question: "So, if I did not put that kind of design in my stories . . . who did?"

I never found out from my grandfather, Arthur Miller, if he shared the Gospel then, but he did recount Garcia's realization at that moment that he had been endowed by a Creator with a specific motivational design expressed in joyful action. This dawning awareness of God as personal Creator was a critical step in Sam's journey to the Christian faith.

Every person comes into the world not as a blank slate but with a unique and innate behavioral orientation. Discovering this pattern is a critical step in vocational discernment because the pattern itself is *already* a kind of primordial call. We are free to choose all kinds of specific actions but not free to disregard the features of our own design. That would be like the proverbial tiger trying to change his stripes. Our choices always and everywhere take place in the context of a given essence, indicating the seeds of our personal vocation. The pattern is the abiding common denominator of one's life, God's basic intention for the person.

AWAKENING TO MOTIVATIONAL DESIGN

My heart leaps up when I behold
A rainbow in the sky:
So was it when my life began;
So is it now I am a man;
So be it when I shall grow old,
Or let me die!
The Child is father of the Man.

—WILLIAM WORDSWORTH—
"My Heart Leaps Up"

"Honey, I didn't feel the baby move today, but as soon as I laid down he hammer fisted my sides and then got quiet again!" This is how my wife, Brooke, described the movement she felt from our first child, David, as he grew inside her. Every day was the same. Long periods would pass when Brooke could barely detect the boy and then, soon after she stretched for sleep, he would vigorously pound two or three times.

Some would be quick to provide mere environmental explanation for this. The baby was just adjusting himself to his mother's new position. Fine. There is surely some truth to that. But then Virginia came along. "She flutters constantly," Brooke would declare. "So different than David! Whether I am walking or lying down I can almost always feel light, gentle movements. No pounding like David."

The pattern of movement from our third child, Nancy, was equally distinct. I remember being astounded one evening as Brooke rested on the couch. "Check this out," she said. I then watched, wide-eyed, as the mountain of her belly seemed to morph into two smaller hills with a valley in the middle. "This child pushes on *both* sides with such strength," Brooke declared. "I feel like I have Samson inside of me!"

The idea that kids arrive as unformed putty just waiting to be molded by parents and society remains sadly prevalent, as Stephen Pinker shows in *The Blank Slate: The Modern Denial of Human Nature*. But any mother or father of multiple kids knows better. Parents do impact their children in either positive or negative ways. That cannot be denied. But the idea that they come into the world *tabula rasa* and end up the "product" of their upbringing is pure nonsense from academics bereft of honest experience with children—or real people, for that matter.

My wife and I have had been blessed with six children. Brooke's experience is that each one of them had a distinctive pattern of movement *in utero*. The early patterns were basic but have become more complex and clearer with each passing year; yet each one's unique personality remains consistent with the way he or she kicked or fluttered or stretched within Brooke. David is intense in whatever he does. Now seventeen, he can focus for hours, but then his movements are explosive—especially on the football field. Virginia, our social and artistic butterfly, gently moves about meeting people and exploring new kinds of creativity. Nancy is powerful and does not like to be contained in the four walls of a house any more than she liked the round constraint of her early home. "Get me out of here!" she seemed to say then, and often says now.

My wife's experience might not be universal. I raise it not

as a scientific proof of motivational design in the pre-born, nor to claim that environmental factors are of no importance to the development of personality, but to indicate an experience widely shared by parents with multiple children: they arrive with their own consistently unique way of being.

Brooke and I have raised each child in the same basic manner. Our relationship remains strong and stable. We worship God and receive the sacraments as Roman Catholics. We are mellower now than seventeen years ago, less prone to freaking out, but our parenting style has not altered significantly. We live in the same part of the country. Our diet has not changed. In fact, with the exception of having more grey hair, the rhythms of our life since David's birth remain largely the same. The primary point is that each kid has come into a common social and family environment, but, from the very beginning, has exhibited an unrepeatable pattern of behavior that is not the result of conditioning.

Although Brooke and I strive to form all our children according to certain general principles—love God and neighbor, be good citizens, observe standard codes of polite etiquette—we are keenly aware each one has his or her own personal vocation that we are responsible for cultivating. The seeds of that calling are present within each one's distinctive motivational design. We do our best to understand that design and to help our kids become aware of it as well. We don't want to squelch discovery or try to define each child too early, for each is a mystery and descriptions always fail to capture the depths of their being. Still, as much as possible, we strive to understand, articulate, and then work "within the grain" of each one's pattern. We try to create conditions in which each child can flourish according to that pattern without undermining basic family unity or sacrificing fairness.

We'll talk more about this custom-tailored approach to formation in forthcoming chapters. For now, let's concentrate on identifying motivational design itself in the context of what we will call the Achievement Story.

TELL ME YOUR STORY

"If we wish to know about a man, we ask 'What is his story—his real, inmost story?'—for each of us is a biography, a story."

—OLIVER SACKS—

We can tell a lot about young people by observing their behavior from the outside. This is the only way parents and caregivers can understand kids for the first years of their lives. As children begin to express themselves at an early age—often in raw, unfiltered ways—we start to understand them from the inside out; they start to tell us their thoughts and feelings. But it takes some years of growing self-awareness in young people before they can articulate deeply their own subjective experience. To *really know* them requires entering into the space of their interior life and seeing the world as much as possible from their perspectives.

In order to truly understand others and move beyond mere external observation we often ask people—young or old—to share their stories. This is a widespread phenomenon transcending cultures of East and West. Precisely because human beings from the dawn of history identify themselves in the context of story, we emphasize it as a critical part of knowing others and helping them grow in self-awareness and effectively discern what they are called to do.

When sharing our stories we often begin by identifying ourselves with broader and recognizable groups of which we are part. Consider some of the ways people respond to the invitation: "Tell me your story." They might start with *family of origin*: "My people are working-class Irish. Mass every Sunday. For most of my family, especially my Dad, it was also the pub every night." Or, connection to *region*: "I'm a Texan! Born and bred. I love hot chili and the Dallas Cowboys!" Kids used to stratified high school environments will often classify themselves by certain types: "I'm a *jock*, a three-sport athlete." "I'm a *gamer*. Mountain Dew and Minecraft every weekend." "I'm a bit of a *nerd*. Give me books and I'm happy." As we grow older we tend to describe ourselves according to *profession*: "I work for General Electric as an engineer. Been there for twenty years." Devout religious persons will often post colors of faith when sharing their story: "I came into the Church on January 4, 1994 and am joyfully Catholic!"

In many ways it is natural and good for us to begin sharing our story with others in broad, objective ways or by identifying with groups of which we are part. Unless trust is built first, we are rightly reluctant to share our interior life. Also, explanation of particular and more personal details of one's self makes more sense in light of overall context. The General Electric employee with a passion for hydropower dams on the Colorado River initially describes himself as an engineer. The young woman who goes on to share the pain of her father's alcoholism first recounts her background in an Irish family where drink was prominent.

Although it is appropriate to reserve deeper explanation of our selves until trust is built and right context is established, our knowledge of one another often remains superficial. The same cultural forces we addressed in Chapter One that undermine personal vocation also apply here. Noise, busyness, and pressure to be disincarnate, conformist consumers all make deep interpersonal encounters difficult, just as such forces undermine the cultivation of unique calling.

Another reason we stop short at general themes of another's story and remain on the outside of interior experience is our tendency to engage in shared interests and common activities. Soccer players talk about the game. Moms share the highs and lows of mothering. Work colleagues discuss the projects they're challenged to finish. And we all discuss the weather.

There is nothing wrong with engaging with one another around shared interests. Indeed, we have deep connection with those who have lived through the same struggles or achieved the same victories. Here our stories intersect. That kind of mutuality is truly a blessing, a point of real solidarity. But what often happens as we interact around *shared experience* is that we miss the other's *own experience*. Knowing one another on the basis of what we have in common is natural, but limited. Too infrequently do we share stories where the richness of interior life is present in vivid color. And yet here is where the "real, inmost story," as Oliver Sacks writes, is found.

THE ACHIEVEMENT STORY

"Whenever a person does something he
or she enjoys doing and does well, the individual
invariably reverts to the same pattern of function-
ing—a unique pattern that is like the individual's
signature."

—ARTHUR MILLER, JR.—
The Power of Uniqueness

We opened this chapter with Sam Garcia's experience recounting activities from his life he had enjoyed doing and believed he had done well. We follow Arthur Miller, Jr. in calling these "achievement stories." Here we will address *what* they are and the motivational design revealed through them. In Chapter Five we will address *how* to effectively draw them out of young people as a critical part of their vocational discernment.

Achievement activities can come from any sphere of activity (school, job, leisure, family, church) or any time of life, but they are not simply passive experiences like soaking up rays on a Florida beach or parking on the couch for eight hours of Jason Bourne movies. They can involve a nearly infinite array of actions because each person is unrepeatable. The activities might involve reaching some contemporary standard of success, like hitting a 4.0 GPA or being the number one sales representative, *but not necessarily*. They might involve a person's satisfaction in rousing applause from an audience but could center on delight in work hidden to all but self and God. They might involve throwing five touchdown passes or composing a harp piece inspired by *The Lord of the Rings* or beating dad in chess or cleaning out the barn or making friends with all the girls in class—any action so long as it brought a deep sense of fulfillment and the person believed he or she did it well.

In a full life account, whether autobiography or biography, we expect details about the major features of that life: major successes or failures, key relationships and connections to well-known historical events. But the most interesting biographies or autobiographies draw out the person's interior life. Without such depth the stories remain two dimensional, flat.

The point of the achievement story is to illuminate a person's unique pattern of motivational design without a full recounting of his or her life. When a geologist wants to understand a piece of land, he drills core samples. He does not need to analyze each square foot because the samples enable accurate assessment of the land's essential elements. Similarly, it is not necessary for us to capture every day of a person's life in order for us to see the essential aspects of his or her motivational design. A series of authentic achievement stories drawn from different periods of a person's life clearly show its recurrence and consistency.

Although achievement stories powerfully reveal a person's motivational design, they are seldom asked for. In my twenty years of experience as a coach, consultant, and teacher, I've worked with thousands of mentees. Maybe five percent of them have ever been asked for their achievement stories at any level of depth. And of these, most have shared their stories as part of a recruitment or personnel development exercise. Very few had the experience of a parent, educator, or pastor asking them to share stories of activities that they deeply enjoyed and believe they did well.

Have you ever had this experience? Have you been asked by an interested other to recount those golden memories of being deeply engaged, fulfilled, and joyful? Have you taken the time with the young people under your care to draw out and truly listen to their achievement stories?

WHERE DOES THIS APPROACH COME FROM?

In the late 1950's, Arthur Miller, Jr. was working alongside a pioneer of modern career counseling, Bernard Haldane. Haldane had noted that individuals express various strengths in their stories of enjoyable activities. Fascinated with this phenomenon, Miller began to look more closely at the auto-biographical narrative and discovered that it expressed not only recurring strengths but also a whole pattern of intrinsically motivated behavior. He called the process of drawing out and describing that pattern the System for Identifying Motivated Abilities® or SIMA®. Most importantly, Miller discovered that beneath the natural strengths of a person there is an underlying drive of core motivation that explains at a natural level *why* people want to exercise those strengths and how they are integrated together.

In Appendix III of this book we list published works by Miller and his associates that provide additional information about motivational patterning as well as books from other fields that corroborate his approach. At this point we highlight two areas of support—one based in Thomistic philosophy and the other in contemporary psychology—that show the value of drawing on achievement stories for understanding the person.

A key principle in the work of St. Thomas Aquinas, which he drew from Aristotle, is that *a being's action reveals its essence.* When we get clear on what a being is most inclined to do, we recognize its nature: "Every living thing gives proof of its life by that operation which is most proper to it and to which it is most inclined" (*Summa Theologiae*, II–II, q. 179). Aquinas mainly employed this principle in describing things at the species level. For example, thoughtful human action indicates an essence of embodied rationality. The action of a falcon in flight indicates the essence of a bird.

The same principle applies at the individual level. We come to know a person by exploring his authentic behavior. Some of our actions are half-hearted and lazy, some are done out of compulsion, some we hate, some we do half-well. These actions where we literally hold ourselves back while "going through the motions" do not reveal who we are in the way deeply fulfilling activities that engage our whole selves do. Stories of engaging action, which shed light on both the interior and exterior life of a person, express a unique essence.

In addition to Thomistic philosophy, evidence from modern psychology lends support to the centrality of achievement stories, often referred to as experiences of "flow." This movement in modern psychology, called Positive Psychology, has been a major part of what Paul Vitz calls "Psychology in Recovery." A general principle of the movement is that we come to know persons and help them to flourish by studying human strength and happiness rather than negative behavior. This starting principle is completely consistent with Arthur Miller Jr.'s approach.

The concept of *flow,* developed by a founder of Positive Psychology, Mihaly Csikszentmihalyi, describes a state of absorption in action that is both challenging and worthwhile. Being in flow is being immersed in any activity that is intrinsically motivating. Stories of "flow state" are nearly identical with achievement stories that reveal a unique pattern of motivation.

TWO STORIES: BENTON & RACHEL

Let's look more closely now at specific examples that show the revelatory power of achievement stories.

Coaching young people as they navigate the waters of major life decisions is a joyful part of my own vocation. I share below two stories from young people I've served. While every mentee's achievement stories reveal a distinctive motivational pattern, Benton and Rachel provide especially clear examples of this phenomenon.

As you read along, pay attention to their core motivational drives. Ask yourself: What orients their behavior? What do they find most fulfilling about the action described?

Benton Parker

Benton recently finished his third year of college, majoring in physics and minoring in music. He is deeply passionate about pursuing a career as a singer/songwriter but is not quite sure how to get there. At the time of this writing, he was uncertain if he should go back to college now or pursue music fulltime. When asked to share his achievement stories, Benton relates a number of memories. Here are a few of them:

Singing Elvis. "My love for singing began when my family took a trip to Graceland outside of Memphis to visit the home of the late, great Elvis Presley—I begged my parents to get his *Greatest Hits* album. My favorite song of his was 'Blue Suede Shoes.' I would beg incessantly for my parents to play Elvis in the car and I almost always sang along, much to the terror of the other passengers."

Portraying the Cowardly Lion. "In second grade I played the Cowardly Lion in our production of *The Wizard of Oz*. I remember being very confident and very particular in the recitation of my lines. After the play, I remember the reception of the performance from my parents being superb, and Ms. Vance, the play's director, was very proud of the job I had done as well."

Playing Recorder. "In fourth grade I was introduced to the recorder. I set for myself the goal of learning the most difficult piece in the songbook: 'The Lion Sleeps Tonight.' I wanted not just to play the song but to memorize it. Towards the end of the semester, we got up in front of the class to play something we had learned and I chose to play that song by memory."

Performing "Smooth." "Junior year in high school I had the solo for Santana's 'Smooth.' I just remembering practicing really hard. I nailed it both in concert and then in band assembly—I *nailed* it."

Performing in a Rock Band in College. "The performance my band and I gave for Rites of Spring was magical. Everything just fell right into place that night, and I can't recall a single mess up by any of us. It feels incredible to have been a part of a group that talented. We gave the audience, our friends, and fellow students a heck of a show."

Mastery, music, and performance. Language never adequately or fully captures a person, but if we had to reduce Benton's motivational pattern to three words these would come very close. His stories do contain other kinds of activities, but "nailing" some kind of musical skill and then performing to an appreciative audience is clearly the dominant theme.

Rachel Michaud

Rachel was a student at Franciscan University of Steubenville and its Center for Leadership, where I am privileged to serve. She graduated with a degree in Catechetics and

Youth Ministry and went on to serve as a missionary with the Fellowship of Catholic University Students (FOCUS). Her achievement stories cover a range of activities.

Participating in Music Ministry. "Singing and music have always been a big part of my family life. When I became old enough, I immediately joined my family in the music ministry at our parish. I am deeply satisfied when I am able to come together with a group and sing something with them that sounds beautiful!"

Playing Rugby and Lacrosse. "I enjoyed pushing myself to develop my skills and really give my all for the team. Being on a team, gelling as a unit, getting to know people's strengths and weaknesses and using that knowledge in order to better work together has allowed me to get to know how people work and how to be a positive influence in their lives."

Serving in High School Leadership Positions. "I enjoyed organizational things: planning retreat experiences, helping to set up for Mass, being involved and in the mix of things, and being a part of the larger community rather than just looking from the outside in."

Volunteering for Catholic Youth Missions. "This was truly one of the highlights of my high school career. I loved forming family bonds with my fellow missionaries throughout my time serving side-by-side with them. I loved being able to lead those younger than me through a retreat experience and being someone that they could look up to."

Serving at Fr. Woody's Haven of Hope. "While serving at Fr. Woody's I did whatever they needed me to do. I really enjoyed getting to interact with the people. One of the biggest blessings of serving there was when I was able to hand a homeless man my Dad's jacket and see what a blessing it was to him. That memory will be forever with me."

Rachel's stories reveal a core drive *to closely participate with others while contributing to their growth*. Her pattern of motivation is more complex than this simple phrase expresses, but the drive to be deeply involved with people while serving with and for them is like a theme song in Rachel's life. It shows up everywhere.

Both Benton and Rachel knew about the presence of their respective motivational drives before I began coaching them. Benton understood well that he loved mastering a song and then "nailing it" during performance. Rachel knew that close involvement with teams was the way she likes to function. This is typical for mentees who are even moderately self-aware. But what surprised both of them, and what most mentees find illuminating, is the constant and consistent presence of motivational design in their behavior and how it orients their approach to everyday living.

Everything we touch with our fingers leaves the mark

of one unrepeatable person. Even identical twins whose genetic structures are virtually indistinguishable have slightly different fingerprints. Our bodies are imbued with distinction from one another. Should we be surprised then that we find in people what the psychologist James Hillman calls the "soul's code," a consistent pattern of intrinsic motivation? In the Christian philosophical tradition, the body is what it is because the soul gives it form. Essential physical differences like genetic structure reflect the shape of the soul.

And just as there are common structures of loops, arches, and whorls in a person's unique fingerprint, so too there are general characteristics of motivational design.

THE NATURE OF MOTIVATIONAL DESIGN

The unique motivational drive of human persons is a deep and abiding natural inclination, not like the power source of a machine that can be switched on and off. Based on achievement stories from tens of thousands of individuals studied through the System for Identifying Motivated Abilities®, several important aspects of the motivational pattern have been revealed.[2]

---

[2] The nature of motivational design is brought out in Arthur Miller, Jr's corpus of work, especially in *The Power of Uniqueness* noted in Appendix III.

The Pattern Is Irresistible

One summer evening over craft beers I spoke with sculptor Dony McManus about the origins of his work as an artist. Dony shared that his mother, also a sculptor, plopped a lump of clay beside him when he was five years old. Since then, sculpting has been an essential part of his life. "I could not do otherwise!" he said.

Although this comment pertains to a very specific professional calling, it captures what is universally true of innate motivational design, our primordial vocation: *We cannot do otherwise.* The patterns of core drives are woven into the fabric of our being. We can channel their energy. We can manage them. We might even stifle their expression for a time or fall prey to circumstances that weaken their energy. For example, jungle lions behind bars at the zoo can become despondent given their limited opportunity to act according to their natural drives. The listless behavior results when their basic and insatiable hunger to be lion-like is denied. Similarly, the innate drive for each one to function according to an inborn pattern of motivational design is irresistible.

If a person cannot find healthy means of living according to this design, he or she will express it in disordered fashion. And, if circumstances lock down the motivation, he or she will be incessantly restless—or, in the worst case, numb with depression. Regardless of environment, a person's hunger to express his or her unique design is irresistible.

When people find in themselves a deep-seated and con-stant hunger to pursue certain kinds of objectives, provided they are inherently positive, they have their finger on God's basic intentionality for their lives.

As early as Dony McManus could remember he loved working with clay to create figures. He "could not do otherwise." Every young person has some basic irresistible drive to be and act in a certain kind of way. It might not be as obvious as Dony's, but every child's unique drive will be present. Paying close attention to it is a critical component of effective vocational discernment.

The Pattern Is Insatiable

Our hunger for food and drink never goes away. We eat and drink and are satisfied for a time. But because we are embodied beings whose bodily existence depends upon food and water, the drive to eat and drink will never be fully satisfied on earth. We are beings whose very nature is defined by the need for sustenance.

Our motivational drives are also insatiable. We never get to the point where our fundamental longing to be a certain way dries up. People never satisfy their motivation in a final way, regardless of how often they have had a chance to express it.

We live in a transient culture where good things come and go. Sometimes my mentees worry whether or not their motivational patterns will go away. "I am like this today, but will I be tomorrow?" "If I commit to one course of action because of motivation, will the drive fizzle out and will I become bored?" Although certain expressions of the pattern might become tedious, the pattern itself does not burn out. I am motivated, for example, to *comprehend a body of knowledge and express my understanding of it* in some way, often by teaching. I love to teach and that will remain an insatiable drive, but I get restless teaching the same class over and over. Knowing that the pattern of motivation is insatiable is important for young people, who are often quite used to the unstable experience of "moving on" from one thing to the next in our liquid culture.

The Pattern Is Enduring

At ninety-four, a man's genetic structure will essentially be the same as it was when he was nine days old. He might be a portly heathen at twenty-five and then become a lean monk at forty-five. Physically and in terms of moral values he might be vastly different from one time of life to another, but his genetic makeup will not fundamentally change. Similarly, motivational design endures. It emerges early in life and remains constant without any fundamental alteration.

This does not mean that persons cannot change or develop. People do change every day. We all find within ourselves a constant restlessness to be more than we are. *But what kind of growth can we achieve and what kind of becoming really satisfies?* If I, as a man, seek the capacity to conceive and bear a child within my body, I will remain profoundly disappointed. Developing wings and flying as a bald eagle is impossible. In growth areas within my reach, such as operatic singing, I might add roundness, volume, and range to my tenor voice, but I'll never naturally reach the deep baritone of a Paul Robeson.

Each one's growth possibilities are oriented by the structure of his or her unique nature. True, the possibilities within that structure are profound! And one's nature does contain a certain degree of plasticity. Through good choices I might forge healthier neurological patterns, for example, but as a forty-four-year-old man I cannot will myself to be a woman or a bald eagle. Nor can I will myself to fundamentally change my pattern of unique motivation. I can either beat my head against this structure or accept it with gratitude.

Knowing that motivational patterns endure without fundamental change has profound implications for vocational discernment. Knowing the structure of their design helps people recognize what God has already called them to be. Benton Parker understands that he is called, at least in part, to seek masterful musical performance because that has been an abiding impulse of his being since grade school. Rachel Michaud, consistently motivated to closely participate with others while contributing to their growth, sees this design as a dimension of her personal vocation. At the same time, motivational patterns also help people see *trajectories of development.* This is invaluable for effectively determining which paths on the horizon authentically fit their unique nature and which are counterfeit.

The Pattern Is Good

As a young Pharisee, Saul (later St. Paul) was a zealous promoter of religious truth. He stirred fellow Jews to persecute followers of Jesus. "[B]reathing threats and murder," he sought permission from the High Priest to track down Christians living in Damascus so that he might "bring them bound to Jerusalem" (Acts 9: 1–2). After a dramatic conversion in which God knocked Saul from his horse and struck him temporarily blind, St. Paul was transformed. Three days later, when he was baptized, St. Paul was grafted into Christ. Saul, the old man, died and became a new man, Paul. And yet his unique nature remained the same. It was elevated and perfected, but not eliminated.

We see the same basic pattern of motivation. He remained a zealous promoter of religious truth but channeled this energy toward exhorting Gentiles to embrace Christianity. After conversion, St. Paul remained a human. He stayed male. He also kept his unique motivational pattern. His nature was created good and remained good after conversion, although now it became integrated into Christ.

It is true that we can do evil with our patterns of motivation. In his pre-Christian days, St. Paul channeled his drive to influence into persecuting others. We sin according to our motivational drives nearly every day of our lives, and yet a strange and beautiful phenomenon occurs in the narration of achievement stories: Mentees tell stories of activities that bring a deep sense of fulfillment and reveal unique motivational designs. The patterns themselves are good. But also (and here is the shocker) *the stories themselves nearly always express good behavior.*

There are some exceptions. My colleague, Rick Wellock, shares the story of a convicted criminal he served as part of Prison Fellowship Ministry. This fellow was motivated to *organize complex processes* and his stories involved running highly sophisticated car thefts. Another man, motivated to *achieve potential*, shamelessly told stories of finding women to seduce in churches because he found them to be more gullible.

However, these kinds of stories are rare in my experience. Even though our culture is saturated with pornography, addiction, infidelity, and binge behavior of all kinds—and even though people gain some degree of pleasure through them—such sinful activities almost never surface in achievement stories.

The reason for this is that actions that are truly fulfilling are also properly ordered. There is a sense of true fit between the person and the activity itself. He or she can declare (and often does): "I was made to do this!" And that experience is invaluable for vocational discernment.

And yet motivational design is not interchangeable with vocation, in the full sense of that word. Motivational design orients the person at the start of his journey without scripting each step along the way. Response to one's calling requires free action. Although motivation inclines us to choose certain directions over others, it is not a cause. Motivation is inherently good, like all of God's creation, but by itself is no sure road to holiness, our universal vocation. It must be baptized, sanctified. Every person must use his or her unique motivational design to make daily decisions to orient themselves toward the glory of God.

Motivation also does not indicate an exact state of life. It does not tell people whether they should marry or whom they should marry. The universal call to holiness, state in life, and daily responses to new challenges and opportunities are all features of personal vocation in its full sense that are influenced but not determined by motivational design.

The Pattern Is Ordered Toward Love

Our desires seek satisfaction. They often express the love of *eros*, which is about the fulfillment of what persons lack. It is *need-based* love.

A person's pattern of motivation expresses need-based love because it is an innate drive to actualize his own potentialities, a drive that includes basic human needs (sought in his own way), as well as inclinations particular to his own unique nature. All my kids seek food and warm clothes in February weather, but only Christopher is my one-man vaudeville show who thirsts for an audience to give him wowed laughter. He springs into the kitchen, twirls around the pillars, and delivers his own version of beat-box rap hoping for hearty engagement with family members. Christopher needs response, desperately.

At the heart of every creature is a deep longing to be fulfilled in accordance with one's own nature. The only being complete in Himself is God. Every other creature, by God's design, lacks what it requires and seeks its own fulfillment. One's pattern of unique motivation orients the person in need-based love to seek the kind of fulfillment proper to him.

At the same time, the pattern of motivation can be a mode of *agape* or self-giving love. I turn again to my son Christopher and his inclination to performance. His exuberant demand for attention and engagement must be managed, but it is inherently good and a source of gift. Recently he acted in an original and slightly zany rock and roll musical, *The Terrible Time Machine of Eloise Mortfellow*. Christopher played the young King Tut. When he emerged on stage clad in gold and riding on a litter, it seemed like everyone in the audience was smiling from ear to ear. As he finished his rap—"Tutankhamen, eat a pound of ramen, the king is a boy, and that's uncommon!"—the crowd erupted. We laughed and cheered and were filled with wholesome pride in Christopher and the other performers who gave of themselves for our delight.

Motivational design is all about love oriented toward fulfillment of self *and* others. When we start out weak and needy in our youth, the pattern is primarily expressed in *eros*. To flourish, Christopher requires food, shelter, and hearty laughter. As a parent, I can love him not only by providing the basics (along with strong educational and spiritual formation), but also by paying close attention to his performances and responding to them with joy.

Motivational design is also oriented toward the fulfillment of others—people making a unique offering of themselves to God and neighbor. Thankfully, Christopher is learning that his own pattern of motivation should be shared to glorify God and build others up. Since motivational design uniquely orients one's heart and soul, it provides the very framework through which he can pour himself out on behalf of others in *agape* or gift-based love.

It is critical, therefore, for mentors to gain an understanding of the motivational designs of the young people under their care. Doing so enables them not only to provide what they uniquely need, but to effectively cultivate and help them orient their unique motivations into a gift of self.

THE PRIMORDIAL VOCATION

We started this chapter with a quote from Bl. Paul VI about the connection between God's design of the person and vocation: "In God's plan, every man is born to seek self-fulfillment, for every human life is called to some task by God. At birth a human being possesses certain aptitudes and abilities in germinal form, and these qualities are to be cultivated so that they may bear fruit." While the Pope does not specify motivation, *per se*, it is a fundamental quality of each person and actually orients his or her aptitudes which are given "in germ." The young girl who exhibits a gift early on for public speaking is naturally inclined for some reason to speak publicly. Aptitudes never show up statically but emerge with a dynamism explained by core motivation. She wants to shape the audience perhaps or confront some injustice or simply communicate her understanding. Motivation undergirds natural aptitude.

The unique design of each person is already a kind of primordial vocation. The fact that it is a structure given when he or she is brought into existence represents a dimension of God's call. Persons must become who they already are. God intends that what is first given "in germ" should take root and flourish. Thus, after the passage with which we started this chapter, Bl. Paul VI goes on to say that the maturing of each one's aptitudes and qualities "will allow each man to direct himself toward the destiny intended for him by his Creator" (*On the Development of Peoples,* no. 15).

The unique motivational design represents the seeds of personal vocation, to which we now turn.

3

PERSONAL VOCATION
The Unrepeatable Word of Every Life
Luke Burgis

"Father, give me a word."
—RITUAL GREETING OF "SEEKERS" TO THE DESERT FATHERS—

AT AGE thirty-eight, Gianna Molla had three beautiful children from three difficult pregnancies. Intestinal dysfunction, excessive vomiting, and prolonged labor pains were the norm for her.

In 1961, Gianna was pregnant with her fourth and final child. The difficulties started early. In her second month, doctors discovered a large fibroma, a type of tumor, in her uterus.

Doctors gave Gianna three options. First, they could remove her uterus—a hysterectomy. This would remove the cancer but result in the death of the baby. Second, they could remove the fibrosis and terminate the pregnancy by abortion in order to lower the risk of future complications. For Gianna, a faithful Catholic, abortion was not an option because it would be the deliberate destruction of a human life. Third, doctors could surgically remove the fibroma alone and allow Gianna to continue an extremely high-risk pregnancy.

Gianna chose the final option—surgical removal of the fibrosis—even though it carried the greatest risk to her own life. Her mission was clear: she was going to bring her child into the world no matter the cost.

At the start of Holy Week in 1962, Gianna was due to give birth any day. Because of the removal of the tumor earlier in the pregnancy, there was a high likelihood of complications. Gianna knew that her life was at risk. She expressed her wishes to her family: "If you must decide between me and the child, do not hesitate: choose the child. I insist on it. Save the baby."

On Good Friday, Gianna's water broke. Her husband Pietro rushed her to the hospital. Doctors tried unsuccessfully to induce labor. On Holy Saturday they performed a cesarean section and delivered a healthy, ten-pound baby girl.

Within a few hours of her daughter's birth, Gianna was in terrible pain. She had septic peritonitis, an infection of the lining of the abdomen, probably as a result of pathogens that spread from her uterus during the C-section.

On Easter Sunday, Gianna used all of her strength to lift her baby girl to her breast and kiss her. Six days later, amid intense suffering, Gianna died. She was thirty-nine years old.

Why did Gianna choose to lay down her life for her child? She had another option—a hysterectomy, if performed with the intention of treating a disease, is not the deliberate destruction of a life, even if it results in the loss of the child as an unintended consequence.

Gianna's choice was not morally necessary. But for Gianna Molla—for the "I" that could only come from her mouth—it *was* necessary. For her, the will of God was not an abstract ideal to be deciphered and weighed—it was a free response of love, the fulfillment of her *personal vocation* in the concrete circumstances of her life. Gianna is a saint not because she made a choice that many others would not have made; she is a saint because she became Gianna Molla. She allowed the love of God to transform her life and fulfill her capacity to love in a very particular way. Gianna's choice was a consequence of her fidelity to living out of her personal vocation.

Gianna's life is a continuous unfolding of a call. As a pediatrician, she worked to support life in its earliest stages. As a mother, she lived—and died—to give that same life. Cardinal Carlo Maria Martini, who presided over Gianna's cause for canonization said that she was a woman who lived her entire life "as a vocation."

Her husband, Pietro, said that Gianna felt bound in conscience to make the choice that she made. Her conscience oriented her to nothing less than the fulfillment of her personal calling. Pope Benedict, speaking about the demands of conscience, wrote, "For man, the will of God is not a foreign force of exterior origin, but the actual orientation of his own being."[1]

Every bone in Gianna's body, every fiber of her being, called her to nurture the life of her child. She didn't count

---

[1] Joseph Ratzinger, *God Is Near Us: The Eucharist, the Heart of Life*, ed. Stephan Otto Horn and Vinzenz Pfnür, trans. Henry Taylor (San Francisco: Ignatius Press, 2003), 104.

the cost. She grasped the inner meaning of her life and never let go.

Personal calling—what we call personal vocation—is like a secret key to discernment. With it, we're able to see and respond to every experience in our lives with an understanding of the way that Jesus is calling us to follow Him *personally*.

Gianna's personal vocation was not revealed only at the end of her life in her heroic act of self-sacrifice. Nor was it "discovered" when she became a pediatrician and then a mother. Rather, it's the reason *why* she became a pediatrician and a mother. Personal vocation is the thread that runs through an entire life from beginning to end.

The mortal remains of St. Gianna Molla reside in a small parish cemetery in Mesero, Italy, near Milan. The epitaph on her grave reads: *Ha offerto l'olocausto della sua vita alla sua maternità* ("She offered a holocaust of her life to her maternity"). In these last words, the *logos*, the truth and order of Gianna's life, is revealed. She gave everything to her vocation as a mother because that's what was asked of her to live out her personal vocation to protect and nurture all life.

Every life carries an unrepeatable "word"—a profound meaning—within it. But will that word ever be spoken? This is our work, and the work of every Christian parent, coach, and educator (and all mentors). We have a responsibility to help cultivate the personal vocations of others. John Paul II says, "this personal vocation and mission defines the dignity and the responsibility of each member of the lay faithful and makes up the focal point of the whole work of formation."[2]

In order to hear the rumblings of each life's unrepeatable word, we have to go back to the beginning. "In the beginning was the Word," writes St. John, and "all things came to be through Him" (John 1:1, 3).

THE CIRCULAR MOVEMENT OF VOCATION

"The *exitus* [going out], or rather God's free act
of creation, is indeed ordered toward the *reditus*
[return] . . . The creature, existing in its own right,
comes home to itself, and this act is an answer in
freedom to God's love."

—CARDINAL JOSEPH RATZINGER (POPE BENEDICT XVI)—
The Spirit of the Liturgy

Did you know that babies babble every possible language? They babble every phoneme, from every language family, as soon as they can make sounds other than crying.

They're created with the capacity for all speech, the potential to say every possible word. Only one really matters, though. It's a word they simply can't hold in: Mom. In the beginning, mom is the *logos*, the entire meaning, of a baby's life.

There's a vibrant paradox here. The child's ability to communicate and express herself well is a function of her

---

2   Pope John Paul II, Post-Synodal Apostolic Exhortation on the Vocation and the Mission of the Lay Faithful *Christifideles Laici*,(December 30, 1988), §58, available from vatican.va (hereafter cited as CL).

limitations. If a baby isn't given a direction in which to develop her capacity for speech—the boundaries of a culture, the choice by her parents not to teach her all of the other 7,000 or so living languages in the world—she'll be a perpetual babbler. But as she learns to speak the handful of words that are essential to her, she begins to enter into a dialogue.

It's the beginning of a lifelong dialogue. *Lógos* creates *diá-logos*, dialogue, and hence communication and communion with others. And the most important dialogue that we enter into is with God, who is the *Logos*, the true Word in which all other words find their meaning.

In his Post-Synodal Apostolic Exhortation on the Word of God, Pope Benedict XVI writes:

> Every man and woman appears as someone to whom the word speaks, challenges and calls to enter this dialogue of love through a free response. Each of us is thus enabled by God to *hear and respond* to his word. We were created in the word and we live in the word; we cannot understand ourselves unless we are open to this dialogue.[3]

The first three chapters of Genesis, when read alongside the prologue of the Gospel of John, present a *logocentric* vision of creation. This is essential to understanding vocation. God created everything through His Word, Jesus Christ. Every creature—each one spoken into existence with

---

[3] Benedict XVI, Post-Synodal Apostolic Exhortation on the Word of God in the Life and Mission of the Church *Verbum Domini*, §22, available from vatican.va (hereafter cited in text as VD).

a unique word—joins its voice together in a great symphony of voices speaking one Word. "Every creature is a word of God, since it proclaims God," writes St. Bonaventure.

We start our lives babbling every possibly word. Then, we make choices that move us in a certain direction. Our movement in this great dance with the Creator gives our lives shape and meaning. We begin to learn the singular Word that called us into existence and continues to call us back to the Father. That *logos* becomes the basis for our dialogue with God.

The Church Fathers, especially St. Irenaeus, spoke of an *exitus-reditus*, a "going forth" and "returning" of all created things to their source. All of creation went out from God; all creation is called back to Him. Thomas Aquinas, taking up the same idea, uses the image of rivers returning to their source. The whole arc of salvation history—Creation, Fall, Redemption, Restoration—is a return of all things to the Father.

With this vision, we can see that the Parable of the Prodigal Son is not only the story of a son returning to his father—it anticipates all of creation returning to the Father. The son, awakened to his true calling, "he came to himself." Then, he freely entered the stream of the *reditus* back to his Father's house.

Pope Benedict writes about the role of free choices in shaping our return to the Father:

This word calls each one of us personally, revealing that *life itself is a vocation* from God. In other words, the more we grow in our personal relationship with the Lord Jesus, the more we realize that he is calling us to holiness in and through the definitive choices by which we respond to his love in our lives. (VD §77)

Vocation is a circular movement because it is a return to the Father, a return to the original *Logos* through whom and for which we were created.

It's the kind of movement that G. K. Chesterton describes in the beginning of his book, *The Everlasting Man*: "There are two ways of getting home; and one of them is to stay there. The other is to walk round the whole world till we come back to the same place."

The place is the same, but the person is not. The journey transforms.

Dynamic Model of Personal Vocation
One Person's Journey

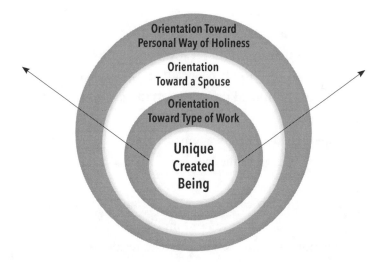

In the Dynamic Model of Vocation (DMOV), a person *goes out* from the center (the core of his being) and arrives at the peripheries. He crosses the outer boundaries and finds himself at home.

There are certain boundaries in his created nature that he must take into account (the boundaries of his "Action Space"), or a general direction that he must take in his journey outward toward the periphery. The order in which he arrives at different layers of his vocation may be different (for instance, he may get married before he embraces a certain type of work), but the movement is the same: it starts at the core and moves outward in the Action Space.

In reality, it's not a two-dimensional journey. But the model illustrates the reality of personal vocation as something rooted in the core of our being, leading us outwards in the movement of the *reditus*. The DMOV doesn't mean that a person simply develops his created nature; it means that a person *responds to the call of God* in an utterly personal way. Let me explain with an example.

My friend Tony has a gregarious spirit and loves the outdoors. He was thrilled to go on snowboarding trips to Big Bear Lake in southern California where he'd insist on being one of the first people on the mountain (which means we'd have to leave at five in the morning) so he could carve fresh tracks. He's also highly motivated to experience and live out his ideals—to give concrete expression to the vision and values that matter to him. He's allergic to peanuts and to people who speak in banal platitudes or start conversations by talking about the weather, and he has a big appetite for risk and adventurous undertakings—on a spring break trip, he was the first one to jump off a rock into the ocean. It's his Created Design.

Yet Tony worked in an accounting office that blasted soul-crushing Muzak every day. He crunched abstract numbers for abstract corporate entities (some of them shell corporations that only existed on paper). He was miserable. Because there was such a misalignment with his core values and way of being, his shadow side started to emerge in order to cope. Tony went to the local bar every night, slammed three or four drinks, and imagined a brighter future. He'd wake up the next morning with a headache and do it all over again. At some point during the day, his girlfriend (a high school sweetheart) would call and speak to him in banal platitudes, telling him to Take It One Day At a Time and repeating things she heard on *Gilmore Girls*.

After a grueling week at the office, Tony was driving along the Pacific Coast Highway in California when he was struck by the beauty of the sunset. He parked his car, walked onto the sandy beach, and took off his shoes. It was a chilly October night. After a few minutes, he felt an urge to get in the water. And so Tony whipped off his tie and walked straight into the cold water in his pinstripe suit until he was waist deep. He let the waves wash over him, and he wept.

Tony describes that experience today as "God's grace washing over him," literally. The next day he quit his job and went to a weekday Mass for the first time in his life.

Over the course of the next year, Tony moved back to South Dakota near the town where he grew up and started a business making wooden furniture. He led workshops for local kids to promote the dying art of craftsmanship. He married a girl, an English teacher in the local high school, who spoke directly and truthfully. He couldn't look at her without thinking about what a beautiful mother she would be. "I never thought that what would attract me most to a woman was her future motherhood," Tony explained.

In Tony's story, we see the outward movement of a created design that led him on his vocational journey through his unique way of responding to God's grace. His trajectory was shaped by his personality, his core motivational drive, and the unique circumstances of his life. He wasn't led *merely* to marriage—a generic state in life—but was oriented toward a specific kind of spouse with whom he could build a healthy and happy family. His motivation to give *concrete expression* to ideas and values found an outlet in his carpentry, an old skill his dad had taught him that was buried under years of corporate conditioning.

Last year, Tony and Cecilia had their first child and Tony finished renovating their new home. His journey of vocation is very different than mine (I have a hard time assembling simple Ikea stuff!), but it's his personal highway to holiness.

Someone on the journey of the *reditus* is like a man setting out from his home in a village at the foot of a mountain, searching for the place his heart longs to be. This place is in his mind's eye, but he doesn't see it anywhere around him. When he looks up at the top of the mountain, though, he thinks, "It must be there."

He begins to wind his way up the mountain—not on a switchback trail, but a circular one that wraps around the mountain over and over again. It's a slow, gradual ascent.

He loses sight of his home every time he wraps around the far side of the mountain.

When he's on the near side of the mountain from which he set out, he can see his home. On most trips, it doesn't look any larger or smaller than it did the last time he passed by. Sometimes, he feels like he's descending rather than ascending. But he continues to walk.

Finally, he finds himself at the top of the mountain, tired and weary. Loop after loop around the mountain is monotonous. He sits down on a rock and looks at the village from which he came. From there, he sees with clarity that the place from which he set out was actually the place he had been searching for the entire time.

On his mission up the mountain, though, he changed. He would never have known his true home, nor appreciated it, nor freely chosen to live in it, had he not taken the journey.

A BRIEF HISTORY OF VOCATION

"For he spoke, and it came to be;
he commanded, and it stood forth."

—PSALM 33:9—

God created the entire universe with our vocations in mind. The idea of personal vocation isn't an invention of Martin Luther, the Second Vatican Council, John Paul II, or Joshua and me. It's the story of creation itself, the adventure of the *exitus-reditus*—our journey back to the Father. It has three major stages: Creation, Confusion, and Convergence.

Creation

The story of vocation starts with creation. The Hebrew verb that describes God's creative work in the first chapters of Genesis is *bara,* a word which always has God as its subject. Only God can create something out of nothing. He creates with his speech: "And God said, 'Let there be light'; and there was light" (Gen 1:3).

God spoke each creature into existence with a unique word that echoes in its being for all eternity, calling it toward the purpose for which it was created. Every creature receives its being in view of a concrete role. When God creates, He calls.

In the New Testament, the Greek word for "calling" is *klésis,* which, like *bara,* refers to a divine act that is always efficacious. Creation and calling are inseparably linked. God creates by calling. We could say that when God created, He *called* the universe into existence. The God who calls us is the same God who created us, and He calls us according to His design. In the case of persons, that design is the *imago Dei,* the image of God.

Every "image of God" is unique and unrepeatable. Because the *imago Dei* is the foundation of human dignity—and because we acknowledge that all people have equal dignity—it's common to think about the image of God as an abstract *sameness* in every person (as if we could just strip the extraneous stuff to find the same mold, the "image of God," hidden underneath every person). Our society tends to equate equality with sameness.

The truth is that each person is a totally unrepeatable image of God, called from the beginning to be "conformed to the image of his Son" (Rom 8:29). By "conform," Paul doesn't mean that each person will *be* the image of the Son, but that each person will assume the shape, the "form" of Jesus Christ, so that each person can be a part of His Body.

Confusion

When God created man in His own image, He gave him a vocation in the same breath: "Be fruitful and multiply, and fill the earth and subdue it; and have dominion over the fish of the sea and over the birds of the sky and over every living thing that moves upon the earth" (Gen 1:28).

Have you ever heard someone say that their calling in life is to be fertile and multiply, to fill the earth and subdue it, and to rule over the fish of the sea and the birds of the sky? Probably not.

But this doesn't mean that the primordial vocation in Genesis is not part of every vocation. Rather, it points to two important realities: First, that God revealed the full meaning of vocation gradually, in history; and second, that every person is called to such a radically unique, personal vocation that every other calling—marriage, family, priesthood, work, multiplying and subduing the earth—does not compete with it, but *subsists* in it.

The word "subsists" means that all of the ways that God calls a person—to a state of life, to a particular kind of work, to holiness—find their meaning in the one personal vocation received by God in the act of creation. There are not multiple vocations any more than there are multiple bodies of Christ. There is one person, called to a unity of life and love.

People use the word "vocation" in many different ways, though, to refer to different aspects of calling. "Personal vocation" is the spirit that animates all of them—the way they are lived out. Personal vocation does not sit beside them: it comes before, after, above, and below them.

When I describe personal vocation, some Catholics immediately stop me and say, "Oh, you are talking about 'little v' vocation, not 'big V' vocation." They usually mean that "big V" vocation (the more important vocation, presumably—because it's big) is "state in life," while 'little v' is some more specific duty inside of it. This is *not* what we are saying! First of all, it's reductionist and confusing to bifurcate vocation into two levels—"little v" and "big V." This implies that there are really two vocations—one more important than the other, or, at best, one lived out "within" or "after" the other one—and it destroys the unity of life that leads one down the path of vocation in the first place. God calls the *whole person*, not the "big Person" and the "little person." Again, personal vocation is the fundamental call that strikes at the heart of the person, without which every other call is unintelligible.

It's helpful to understand all of the ways that people use the word "vocation." Here are the most common ways that the word is used:

Vocation as Being. Pope John Paul II said, "Every life is a vocation."[4] All of created reality has an eternal vocation— even the sun and stars—because God's redemption extends to all matter. Nothing is created without a purpose. From the first moment of its existence, each thing has an "end" to which it is called. Abortion is always the loss of a vocation: a unique, unrepeatable life, destined to manifest the glory of God in a singular way. That life is destroyed in the womb by an adult who can't see a person, let alone a vocation. Nothing is called into existence without a vocation.

Vocation as Self-Actualization. In the secular world, the concept of self-actualization, or achieving one's full potential, is often couched in vocational terms. It's part of the American psyche, from the U.S. Army's slogan, "Be All You Can Be," to the ideal of the "self-made man," epitomized at one time by John D. Rockefeller. There is truth in self-actualization to the extent that, in our creative freedom, we have the power to shape our lives within certain bounds. But this individualistic idea of fulfillment lacks all sense of communion, of love, and of the supernatural end to which we're called.

Vocation as the Universal Call to Holiness. All of the baptized are called to be saints. In every state of life, God calls people to live the heroism of ordinary life, investing all of their actions with love. This makes them extraordinary. In 1930, Pope Pius XI wrote:

---

[4] Pope John Paul II, Address at World Youth Day, 2001

> For all men of every condition, in whatever honorable walk of life they may be, can and ought to imitate that most perfect example of holiness placed before man by God, namely Christ Our Lord, and by God's grace to arrive at the summit of perfection, as is proved by the example set us of many saints.[5]

Vocation as State in Life. This is the most common usage of the word "vocation" among Catholics. It refers to four traditional states in life: marriage, priesthood, religious life, or single life. No doubt these basic commitments in life orient and put boundaries around one's actions in the world (in the best possible way)—they are the way of love that a person walks. A married man can look at his wife's face and think, "She is my pathway to heaven." A priest could think the same when he picks up his breviary, celebrates the Mass, or listens to the penitent sitting in front of him in the confessional. But "state in life" does not constitute the totality of a vocation. It is simply the "state" in which one is called to live and love.

Vocation as Work or Task. Many people feel called to dedicate themselves to a specific job, task, or ministry. This can certainly be part of God's call. It's dangerous to associate vocation only with *doing*, though.

In the early twentieth century, the sociologist Max Weber popularized the idea that the Protestant work ethic

---

5 Pope Pius XI, Encyclical Letter on Christian Marriage *Casti connubii* (December 31, 1930), §23.

was the virtuous driver of capitalism. Karl Barth, the great reformed theologian, pushed back strongly against this notion, warning that the identification of "vocation" with "profession" could easily lead to secularization. He was right. Work becomes a pathway to holiness only when it maintains its "vertical horizon," contributing not only to the improvement of the material world but also to the *sanctification* of the world.

If a tow truck driver—even if he isn't aware of a particular "call" to be a tow truck driver—is able to sanctify his work by doing it with love, then it acquires a salvific and redemptive value, above and beyond the value of a towed car. If you've had your car towed recently, you may think that's impossible. But I assure you that there's a tow truck driver out there who prays for every person whose car he tows and invests so much love into his work, which he does to support his growing family, that he's becoming holy. And when he gets home at night and drinks a Coors Light with his wife, God delights in him.

These senses of vocation have jockeyed for position over the years. In Sacred Scripture, it would seem that only a select few people were called by God to some specific task: the prophets, the judges, Moses, and a few other "chosen ones." What about everyone else? Here we need to make a critical distinction between an objective call from the Creator and the subjective *awareness* of that call. All have been called to a personal vocation in the very act of creation, but not all are fully conscious of what it is. And that's okay. Because even when we don't know how to speak the word at the center of our soul, the Holy Spirit does. "[T]he Spirit helps us in our weakness; for we do not know how to pray as we ought, but the Spirit himself intercedes with sighs too deep for words" (Rom 8:26), writes Paul.

In the Gospels, Jesus clearly has a personal vocation. His vocation is not "the single life" or "carpentry"—these are the reductionist categories we might assign to a single carpenter today. Fr. Herbert Alphonso, S.J., believed that Jesus' personal vocation could be summed up in one word, "*abba*," which signifies His relationship to the Father. Germaine Grisez and Russell Shaw suggest that Jesus' personal vocation was "savior." I think that his personal vocation on earth was something more concrete, something which contains both of those things: *the Cross*. All of the Gospels read like a movement toward the Cross, the culmination of His work as "savior." And it is on the Cross that Jesus utters the word "*abba*" for the last time. He was on the Cross because He was doing his Father's will. The Cross is the lens through which we can understand His entire life. In other words, His personal vocation.

For St. Paul, the concept of personal vocation is rooted in the doctrine of charisms and the Church as the Body of Christ:

> For as in one body we have many members, and all the members do not have the same function, so we, though many, are one body in Christ, and individually members one of another. Having gifts that differ according to the grace given to us, let us use them. (Rom 12:4–6)

In the early Church, the baptismal call was central to the understanding of vocation. Each person was called to the "obedience of faith," following Christ in the unique circumstances of his life. This led to martyrdom for many. In the *Epistle to Diognetus*, a beautiful defense of Christianity written by an unknown author in the first few centuries after Christ, it is written: "The Christian is to the world what the soul is to the body." In the living out of their lives, Christians gave a Christ-like "form" to the pagan society in which they lived.

In the centuries that followed, differences between "states in life" started to be emphasized. This coincided with the birth of monasticism, led by St. Anthony of the Desert (AD 356) and St. Benedict of Nursia (AD 547). The priest, monk, or religious was thought to be on the path to Christian perfection, while those who remained "in the world" settled for something less than holiness. Unfortunately, this dichotomy persisted throughout the Middle Ages until the Protestant Reformation.

Martin Luther believed that every person was called to live out their vocation in the world, in the midst of work and family. During the Reformation, there was an affirmation of ordinary life. According to Luther, the fabric of individual lives constituted the "knowledge of faith in which all saints are instructed, each one in his own vocation."[6] With his strong polemics, Luther took a battering ram to the hierarchically-structured vocations and placed

---

6   Martin Luther, "The Judgment of Martin Luther on Monastic Vows, 1521," in *Luther's Works*, American Edition, 55 vols. Eds. Pelikan and Lehmann (St. Louis: Concordia and Fortress, 1955–86), Vol. 44, 269.

sole emphasis on the personal calling of every person in the world.

There was a major problem. Since Luther rejected all forms of mediation in the spiritual world (and with it, the priesthood and religious life), the Catholic Church reacted to him by emphasizing the critical role of vocations to the priesthood and religious life. As a consequence, in the centuries after the Reformation, the word "vocation" came to be associated almost exclusively with "state in life" in the minds of many Catholics. In some cases, Catholics use it to refer *only* to the priesthood and religious life. Sadly, this still happens today. When a Catholic priest implores people to pray for an "increase in vocations," most think that what he *really* means is to pray for an increase in priests and religious. This is a very impoverished way of looking at vocation.

There is an urgent need for a strong, well-developed theology of vocation that takes seriously the personal calling of each member of the Body of Christ as something unique and necessary in God's plan, while still acknowledging that God calls certain people to different hierarchical roles within the Church.

Fortunately, over the past sixty years, we have started to see the many streams of vocation converge into the rich reality that we call "personal vocation."

Convergence

In the years leading up to the Second Vatican Council, many prophetic voices sensed the importance of personal vocation. St. Ignatius of Loyola, St. Frances de Sales, and Jean-Pierre de Caussade, S.J., each emphasized the primacy of God's personal call in discernment. In the twentieth century, St. Josemaría Escrivá understood the reality of personal vocation as something rooted in our being, which illuminates all of our choices. In *Christ is Passing By*, he writes

> Our calling discloses to us the meaning of our existence. It means being convinced, through faith, of the reason for our life on earth. Our life, the present, past and future, acquires a new dimension, a depth we did not perceive before. All happenings and events now fall within their true perspective: we understand where God is leading us, and we feel ourselves borne along by this task entrusted to us.[7]

The Second Vatican Council made the teaching about personal vocation explicit, especially in its document *Lumen Gentium*, the Dogmatic Constitution on the Church. The Council Fathers wrote, "All the faithful of Christ of whatever rank or status, are called to the fullness of the Christian life and to the perfection of charity." This is the universal call to holiness. Each person, though, has a specific way to grow in holiness. They continued: "In order that the faithful may reach this perfection, they must use their strength accordingly as they have received it, as a gift from Christ."[8]

---

[7] Josemaría Escrivá, *Christ is Passing By* (New York: Scepter Publishers, 2010), no. 45.

[8] Second Vatican Council, Dogmatic Constitution on the Church *Lumen Gentium* (November 21, 1964), §40.

Every pope since the Second Vatican Council has spoken in his own way about the reality of personal vocation. Perhaps none did so more forcefully than Pope John Paul II. Before he became pope, he wrote in his book *Love and Responsibility* that "'vocation' indicates that there exists a proper direction of every person's development through commitment of his whole life in the service of certain values."[9]

In his encyclical, *On the Redeemer of Man*, Pope John Paul II calls each person "the way for the Church," each with a unique and unrepeatable way of being united to the Lord (RH §14). In many other places (*Christifideles Laici, Pastores Dabo Vobis*, and others) he lays out a strong vision of the responsibility that every member of the Christian faithful has to cultivate his or her own personal calling and to help others to do the same.

Pope Benedict XVI had such fidelity to his personal vocation that he was able to resign from the papacy when he became convinced that abdicating was what the Lord was calling him *personally* to do—even when no pope in over six hundred years had done the same.

In his writings, Pope Benedict wrote about why the relationship between the laity and the clergy is essential to the development of personal vocation:

Every person carries within himself a project of God, a personal vocation, a personal idea of God on what he is required to do in history to build his

---

[9] Karol Wojtyla, *Love and Responsibility*, trans. Grzegorz Ignatik (Boston: Pauline Books & Media, 2013), 242.

Church, a living Temple of his presence. And the priest's role is above all to reawaken this awareness, to help the individual discover his personal vocation, God's task for each one of us.[10]

We are united in our common calling to build the Church, the Body of Christ, on whatever path God has called us to.

THE COMMON ELEMENTS OF EVERY CHRISTIAN VOCATION

"Has it ever occurred to you that one hundred pianos all tuned to the same fork are automatically tuned to each other?"

—A.W. TOZER—

The Pursuit of God:
The Human Thirst for the Divine

Orchestras always tune to "A." In the great symphony of being, every creature—each with its own voice—is tuned to Christ. Every personal vocation is rooted in the following six dimensions of the Christian calling:

Trinitarian. The Trinitarian dimension of vocation, received at Baptism, allows a person to return to the Father, in the Son, through the Holy Spirit, in the movement of the *reditus*.

---

[10] Pope Benedict XVI, Pastoral Visit to the Parish of St. Felicity and Her Children, Martyrs, Fifth Sunday of Lent (March 25, 2007), available from vatican.va.

Apostolic. Every vocation has an apostolic, missionary dimension of transmitting the faith, making known to others the reality of Trinitarian love, and cultivating the unique, personal vocations of others to build up the Body of Christ.

Christification of the Cosmos. Human persons are the voice of all of creation. In our priestly role as baptized Christians, we offer created reality to the Father and give a Christological form to the world. For those who work in business, their desk is an altar. For those who work on a farm, the soil is the place of offering.

Soteriological. Every vocation is *saving* insofar as it is a cooperation with Christ in the redemption of the world. A vocation is a person's unique call to contribute, with their life, in the return of everything to the Father, offering their life as a sacrifice pleasing to God, completing "what is lacking in Christ's afflictions for the sake of his body, that is, the Church" (Col 1:24).

Ecclesial. Every vocation is lived out in the Church and builds up the Body of Christ. For a Catholic, a vocation is nourished by the sacraments, especially the Eucharist. Since a vocation is not only about self-actualization but the good of the whole Body, it can never be discerned solely as an individual, apart from the Body.

The Tria Munera. Referring to the three-fold ministry of every Christian as priest, prophet, and king, the final dimension of vocation is the Tria Munera. As priests, we offer all of creation to the Father, with the Son, in the Holy Spirit. As prophets, we bear the truth of God to the world. As kings, we're called to govern our lives (and families) by directing everything toward God (CCC 783–786).

CALL TO AUTHENTIC LOVE

Love, it will not betray you
Dismay or enslave you, it will set you free
Be more like the man you were made to be

—MUMFORD & SONS—
"Sigh No More"

Personal vocation is such a rich reality that no single definition or meaning can sum it up completely. It is the way that each unique person was created and called to give and receive love in the world. It *frees* us to love others with our whole heart, our whole mind, and all of our strength. It is our authentic, personal way of loving God and neighbor, and it illuminates our pathway back to the Father in all its varied states and forms.

According to Fr. Herbert Alphonso, S.J., there are three core aspects of personal vocation:

Personal Union with Christ

Every personal vocation finds its ultimate meaning in Jesus Christ, the *Logos* through whom all things were created. Each person sees Jesus' face in a unique way, and each is united to Him in a way that no other person has been or ever will be. That's because it is only our authentic self that can be united with the person of Jesus. He wants us—the real us—and not our illusions or fantasies about who we are. We are far more unique than our fantasies.

Pope John Paul II, in his encyclical *On the Redeemer of Man*, speaks about what each person must do in order for this personal union to take place:

> [Each person] must, so to speak, enter into him with all his own self, he must "appropriate" and assimilate the whole of the reality of the Incarnation and Redemption in order to find himself. If this profound process takes place within him, he then bears fruit not only of adoration of God but also of deep wonder at himself. (RH §10)

There are many ways to do this, but all of them start with taking your entire self seriously—your strengths, weaknesses, hopes, dreams, fears, anxieties, and joys.

When I was in my late twenties, I stepped away from my work as an entrepreneur in order to be completely open to the possibility of the priesthood. During my first days of seminary formation, a retreat director asked us: "Who is Jesus to you?" I balked because I thought the idea of a personal Jesus sounded subjectivist. My first thought was, "Jesus is Jesus! He is who He is." And that is true. But in my smugness—in my attempt to push back against anything that smelled of relativism—I was missing the point.

The resurrected Lord *does* have a totally unique relationship with every baptized person in the world. We can each say, truly, "My Jesus is like *this.*" Because our union with the Lord is unrepeatable and unique, we see a certain side of Jesus that others have not experienced, fruit of the personal bond of love that we share.

Every baptized Christian has a responsibility to manifest that aspect of Christ's infinitely rich personality, which only he has experienced, to the rest of creation.

Unique Meaning

All superhero movies are really vocation stories, and the most popular of them all are origin stories. Why do we like these stories so much?

Batman Begins opens with Bruce Wayne playing with his childhood friend in the yard at Wayne Manor when he falls down a dry well full of bats. The scene is chock-full of meaning about the person of Bruce Wayne, revealing more about him than every other Batman movie combined. The circumstances of his early life—his fall into a dry well full of bats, the murder of his parents, his grappling with justice in a Bhutanese prison camp—all played a role in the development of who he would become. *Batman Begins* is not simply "a vocation story" (as if all superheroes had the same vocation) but the story of a personal vocation. It explains why Bruce Wayne became a very specific superhero.

Now what would happen if the Batsuit, the Batmobile, and all of his gadgets were suddenly taken away? What would happen if Batman eradicated all of the crime in Gotham city? What would he do?

This is the true test of a vocation. When everything

is stripped away and all of our functions are gone, are we still ourselves? Do we have a vocation that is rooted in our being? If we don't, we'll be in total crisis.

A vocation that is rooted in who we are rather than what we do allows us to find meaning in the midst of every circumstance of life. Viktor Frankl, an Austrian neurologist and psychiatrist, was a prisoner in the Nazi concentration camp of Auschwitz during the Holocaust. The different titles that he had built his identity around—neurologist, psychiatrist, husband, brother, friend—were different now. The same was true of every other person in Auschwitz.

Frankl quickly realized there was one thing that could never be taken away: the unique, God-given meaning for which each person lived. He noticed that those who had forgotten their unique meaning were wasting away, dying physically and psychologically. He worked with them to help them discover the meaning for which they lived.

In other words: he helped them discover their unique, personal vocations.

Integration

Personal vocation impels us toward integrity and unity of life. It prevents us from living a scattered, siloed existence in which we seem to have one vocation at work, another vocation at home, and another on Sundays. Our personal vocation is the reality that allows us to do only one thing at all times. It's our one thing necessary.

Jesus' one thing necessary was His Father's will. In fulfilling His personal vocation, he was walking the path of the *reditus* on which he would return to the Father. His pathway was the *Via Crucis*, the Way of the Cross, on which "having loved his own who were in the world, he loved them to the end" (John 13:1). When there were competing demands in His life, Jesus always knew what He had to do. He would not return to the Father until His mission was complete.

There's great freedom in embracing our personal vocation. It helps order our desires and allows us to act confidently in accordance with them. When the world presents us with competing values, we're not totally perplexed or paralyzed—we know what we need to do. Those competing forces in the world do not pull us apart because we are living in the integrity of our call.

Living out our personal vocations gives us tremendous freedom to love in the way that only we are called to love. It gives us the freedom to be about the business that God entrusted to us, and not to worry about the business that he entrusted to everyone else. Here's the beauty: He gave personal vocations to the other seven-and-a-half billion people in the world, too. We can rest easy knowing that He asks us only to be faithful to our own. In the freedom of our unique vocation, we can flourish.

The Freedom to Love: A Promise

In our work cultivating vocations, we must be humble enough to recognize the radically personal way that God calls each individual. If we stop thinking of vocations in terms of "categories" and focus on the unique person who is at the heart of every vocation, we will see a flourishing of people embracing and living out all vocations.

There is an external aspect to every call. The Church calls in and through her members—the lay faithful, bishops, priests, vocation directors, and all others. The role of the Church is not to call louder and louder but to listen closer and closer, helping every person respond in love to the word that God is speaking in the depths of their heart.

We must be both interested and disinterested. We have to be interested in every person's authentic personal vocation, without exception, wherever it may lead. We also have to be disinterested and not pull for a vocational choice based on our own self-interest or what we think might be in the interest of the Church. God knows what His Church needs, and He is intensely interested in every person.

It's easy to sniff out people with a personal agenda. Many young Catholics will not even start a conversation with a Vocation Director—even if they do feel a vague pull to priestly ministry or religious life—because its websites, videos, and brochures all suggest that it exists for the sole purpose of cultivating priestly and religious vocations. They think, "Well, God *might* be calling to me to be a priest . . . but if I start down that path, are they going to put on the full court-press, woo me like a five-star college recruit, and push me toward a certain path?" This is tragic. Shouldn't our vocation directors be concerned with *all vocations*?

If we would turn our focus to the unique, personal vocation of each person—if we embrace the full meaning of vocation—there will *naturally* be more priests and religious. There's no shortage of vocations. There's only a shortage of people living them out. When young people sense that we are interested in their journey, whether it leads them to a seminary or to a baseball diamond, they're more open, honest, and free. Each of them is the "Way for the Church." We have to walk down every way.

We will find that each of these ways lead to a beautiful place—to God Himself—if we're willing to follow it to the end.

THE LAST WORD

"Maria, All the beautiful sounds of the world in a
single word . . .
Say it loud and there's music playing;
Say it soft and it's almost like praying . . . "

—"Maria"—
West Side Story

Early in the morning on the first day of the week, Mary Magdalene comes to the tomb where Jesus is buried. She finds the stone rolled back and the tomb empty and stands outside weeping. One of the two angels at the tomb asks her why she's weeping. "Because they have taken away my Lord, and I do not know where they have laid him" (John 20:13), Mary answers. She speaks as if it was *her* Jesus, her Lord, who she is looking for. She had a unique relationship with Him—as did Peter and Andrew, James and John, Lazarus and Martha.

When the risen Jesus appears to her, she mistakes Him for the gardener. Worse yet, she mistakes Him as the number one suspect in the theft of a body. "Sir," she says, "if you have carried him away, tell me where you have laid him, and I will take him away." Jesus, looking at her lovingly, says one word: "Mary."

That was enough for her. Instantly, Mary recognizes that she's talking to Jesus. "*Rabboni!*" she cries, and clings to Him.

The Evangelist records this exchange in Hebrew—"*Miriam!*" . . . "*Rabboni!*"—to preserve the unrepeatability of a personal encounter. An exchange of information is repeatable. But a tone of voice, the shape of a smile, the gleam in an eye, and the joy in a countenance: these things belong to an encounter between persons.

It's in the process of living out a personal vocation that a real transformation in Christ takes place. Mary lived out all three dimensions of hers: the Christological, the meaningful, and the integral. She clung to Jesus—*her Jesus*—and was united to Him in a singular way. She found her deepest source of inner meaning in Him, the *why* that allowed her to endure any *what*. And she had been made whole. The Lord had given her back the pieces of her scattered life. In loving her wholly, He allowed her to love deeply and authentically in return, from the core of her being.

Mary recognized the Lord in her personal vocation. The French writer and philosopher Fabrice Hadjadj sums this up in his book of meditations on the resurrection:

Mary does not recognize Jesus by his famous face or even by his voice. She recognizes him by her vocation. What matters is not an external, common image, but an interior, personal echo. He calls her by her own name and entrusts to her the task of transmitting to the others her testimony of this incommunicable face-to-face encounter. And this is why the others, to begin with, cannot bring themselves to believe her. The Good News escapes the parameters of news: it is not information for everyone, but a call to each.[11]

Mary heard her name called personally by the Lord. After babbling every possible word as a baby, after her heart was stifled from crying out during her years of use and abuse by others, after slowly learning the *logos* of her life and the personal invitation to become the person she was created to be, she was finally able to speak that one word that made her heart leap when it left her lips: *Rabboni.*

'Till the End

C. S. Lewis wrote a book called *Till We Have Faces*, which could've just as easily been called *Till We Have the Words to Say.* Near the end of the book, after the main character, Orual, has spent her life trying to figure out why she has never understood the ways of the gods, she reflects:

When the time comes to you at which you will be forced at last to utter the speech which has lain at the center of your soul for years. . . . Till that word can be dug out of us, why should [the gods] hear the

---

[11] Fabrice Hadjadj, *The Resurrection: Experience Life in the Risen Christ.* (New York: Magnificat, 2016), loc. 645, Kindle.

babble that we think we mean? How can they meet us face to face till we have faces?

When we discover and live out our personal vocation, we will, at the end, speak the singular word that lies at the center of our soul from the beginning, the "new name written on the stone which no one knows except him who receives it" (Rev 2:17).

Fr. Alphonso, author of the book *Personal Vocation*, shares a little-known poem by T. S. Eliot called *The Naming of Cats*. A cat has three names, Eliot writes. First, there's the name that the family uses every day. Second, there's a particular name that never belongs to more than one cat, a peculiar and more dignified name like Munkustrap, Quaxo, or Coricopat. But there is still one name left over.

And that is the name that you never will guess;
The name that no human research can discover—
But the cat himself knows, and will never confess.
When you notice a cat in profound meditation,
The reason, I tell you, is always the same:
His mind is engaged in a rapt contemplation
Of the thought, of the thought, of the thought of
      his name:
His ineffable, effable,
Effanineffable
Deep and inscrutable singular Name.

The name left over—the deep and inscrutable singular Name—is the "new name written on the stone which no one knows except him who receives it," the name by which we were called from the beginning . . . our personal vocation.

4

MENTORING WITH EMPATHY

Joshua Miller

"If we are to love our neighbors, before doing
anything else we must see our neighbors. With our
imagination as well as our eyes, that is to say like
artists, we must see not just their faces but the life
behind and within their faces. Here it is love that is
the frame we see them in."

—FREDERICK BUECHNER—
Whistling in the Dark: A Doubter's Dictionary

GETTING TO KNOW MENTEES

HUMAN BEINGS always faced the challenge of getting
to know one another deeply. Today the difficulty seems
especially great. We're busy. We're transient. Wanderlust
or the need to move interrupts relationships. Distractions
abound. Advances in computer technology enable frequent
opportunities to "connect" but often screen out the body
language and tone of voice which some experts say account
for 50 to 80 percent of real communication. We hunger for
deep relationships, but often try to build them on an anemic

diet of texts and emails versus the richness of true face-to-face interaction.

Even parents who live with their children for eighteen years before they leave the nest can have difficulty getting to know them. In the frenetic busyness of meeting their children's myriad needs, parents sometimes fail to inquire and listen with empathy, and thus truly see the authentic nature of their kids.

It's hard getting to know others. If we want to help them become who they were created to be, though, it is imperative that we do so. Our Triune God is relational. We image Him. We are called by virtue of that fundamental reality to be relational, to know others and be known by them.

In this chapter we will discuss how loving empathy—expressed by asking the right kinds of open-ended questions and listening attentively—can significantly help mentors get to know their mentees well and build the kind of relational context in which effective vocational mentorship can take place. These questions also enable mentors to build rapport *more quickly* and get to know their mentees. Windows of opportunity are often brief. Young people move on quickly and often have limited attention. We need to use the time we are given with them effectively.

What do people mean when they talk about knowing the other?

Sometimes they mean mere acquaintance. Where I live in Ohio, perfect strangers will often say, "Good to know you," when introduced to one another. Familiarity through social connections can make the encounter more meaningful. "Yeah, I know Deanna. She was my brother's girlfriend back in high school." Obviously there are various ways of knowing another person. We are not going to explore the meaning of knowing in depth—thousands of books have been written on epistemology, the study of knowledge. For our purposes, knowing another person means developing a relationship with that person and perceiving the truth or nature of that person to some degree.

But what is it about a person that is most true of them?

First, *relationships.* A person's relationships—especially those that are most foundational and enduring—constitute an important part of the person. We find ourselves within a rich web of relationships. One person is at the same time a daughter of God, a child of Edith and William, the wife of Arthur, the mother of Jacob, a friend of Carrie, and so on. We each have our own concrete individuality, but relationships literally define who we are.

Second, *essential characteristics.* We describe people according to general traits that they share with all other people (embodied rationality) or with many (extroversion or introversion), but these characteristics don't reveal the unrepeatable nature of the person, which can't be captured with language. "Peaceful" and "calming" are accurate descriptions of my wife's voice as she sings Gregorian Chant, but I can use those words to describe how others sing. Her way of singing, and of being in general, is her own. As much as possible, we need to encounter others and see them according to their unrepeatable selves.

In common speech we often ask, "What is your story?" There's a lot of wisdom embedded in that question. A person's relationships and essential characteristics come alive in his story. Stories allow us to see one's intrinsic energy to be a certain way in a social, cultural, historical, and familial context. We see others acting upon him, and his self-creative freedom in responding to those actions. His story connects this dynamic exchange in a holistic way.

We reveal ourselves to others when we share our stories with them, especially when we reveal the most meaningful actions of our lives. Telling the journey of dating and then marrying our spouses lets others into our world more so than tales of first encounters with a musician or a new recipe for Cajun gumbo. At the same time, the very process of formulating meaningful stories is important because it enables us to become more deeply aware of who we are.

Mentors gain rich knowledge when they draw out the authentic story of their mentees while also providing them an important opportunity for growth in self-understanding, which is a critical part of cultivating personal vocation.

The key to effectively drawing out those stories is empathy. When mentors listen with empathy, they foster authentic development in their mentees. Empathy, as we will see, is like sun and gentle rain to the young sapling. It fosters growth.

EMPATHY

*"It is an absolute human certainty that no
one can know his own beauty or perceive a sense
of his own worth until it has been reflected back
to him in the mirror of another loving, caring
human being."*

—JOHN JOSEPH POWELL, S.J.—
The Secret of Staying In Love

When mentors ask good questions that evoke thoughtful reflection, they demonstrate sincere interest in knowing their mentees. Such questions, born of empathy, orient mentees to share themselves authentically. Empathic listening is the corresponding skill that enables mentors to truly understand their mentees intellectually and emotionally. Beyond the value of understanding, empathic inquiry and listening have the further effect of actually fostering the growth of mentees who delight in being received and affirmed in their personhood.

In this section we first define empathy and then unfold its two-fold movement of reaching out (asking good questions) and actively receiving (listening deeply). We then consider empathy as manifested in the Lord Jesus as a model and imperative for His disciples to follow.

First, what do we mean by empathy?

The Oxford Dictionary provides a clean, clear definition: "The ability to understand and share the feelings of another." The word emerges from the Greek *empatheia,* from the root *pathos,* or feeling. The Greek prefix *em* means "in" or "to go into." Through empathy we go into the feelings of the other. And yet it is not a purely emotional experience. We *understand* and *share* the feelings of the other when we empathize with them. We get where they are coming from. We see the world from their perspective.

Empathy does not always involve agreement, though. That's *sympathy*. Sympathy comes from the Greek prefix *sym*, which means "with," "together," and feeling with the other in the sense of agreement. For example, I might sympathize with coal miners frustrated with poor working conditions and agree with the position they take against company management. Sympathy can also express common feeling that assumes agreement. For example, as my family and I left the funeral for Grandad Miller, our hearts were knit together in sympathy, thanksgiving, and celebration of his life.

Sympathy is often right and proper, but it is not the same as empathy. It is very possible and indeed necessary for human relationships that we enter into the feelings of others—stand in their shoes, see the world from their perspective—without making those feelings our own or adhering to their positions. We might with good reason come to the same emotional or intellectual stance as another, but it is critical to do so with self-possession, a key mark of authentic personhood.

A two-fold movement occurs in empathy. First, there is transcendence of one's self in order to reach into the experience of another person, while remaining firmly anchored in self-possession. The second movement is the opening up of space in one's self for the other and actively receiving him.

Jesus Christ gives us the supreme example of this two-fold movement of empathy. *First, the Incarnation itself is divine empathy.* St. Irenaeus declared that Jesus "became as we are in order that we might become as he is." Irenaeus does not use the word "empathy," but he expresses the same reality: Christ entered into and shared the life of men. From His intimate communion in the Blessed Trinity, Jesus took on human flesh and entered into human history. He did not enter into our sin, but truly shared in the experience of our earthly sojourn in a fallen world. Precisely because of the divine empathy of the Incarnation, Christ opens a way for human beings to gain intimate relationship with God. He calls us friends and He opens His heart to us so that we may "become partakers of the divine nature" (2 Pet 1:4).

In Christ we see the two-fold movement of empathy. He enters into our experience and provides space for us to enter into His life. There is an especially poignant example of this in the eleventh chapter of the Gospel of John. Jesus hears of His friend Lazarus' illness and He goes to Bethany where Lazarus lives with his sisters Martha and Mary. Before Jesus can even enter the village, Mary runs out to meet Him. She falls at His feet, and the following encounter takes place:

> "Lord, if you had been here, my brother would not have died." When Jesus saw her weeping, and the Jews who came with her also weeping, he was deeply moved in spirit and troubled; and he said "Where have you laid him?" They said to him, "Lord come and see." Jesus wept. (John 11:32–35)

The Lord is well aware that He has the power to raise Lazarus from the dead and will do so soon. His response could be: "This is not a problem. Clearly you don't have enough faith. Just wait a minute." But that kind of response, although true, would not have acknowledged the feeling and experience of Mary. Instead, Jesus shared her distress. He wept as she wept. He loved Mary with the kind of love that was called for. Through His divine empathy, He entered into her experience and loved her in the midst of her sorrow.

We are called to imitate Christ. And imitating Christ in His love *necessarily* involves being empathic—entering into the lives of others, especially those whose personal vocations we are called to cultivate. We must make space for them in our hearts, understand them intellectually and emotionally, and thus love them in the warm and welcoming context of the empathic embrace.

Empathy is rare. Our educational system instructs us in how to write, read, and speak. Classes abound in these areas. But have you ever seen a class at any level of the educational spectrum devoted to empathic inquiry and listening? Although the great majority of what is communicated in human interaction is perceived through sensitivity to body language and vocal tone, we still fail to emphasize its value.

How do we as mentors become more empathic?

CLOSED, LEADING, AND OPEN-ENDED QUESTIONS

Effective mentors ask a variety of good questions in service to their mentees. There is a proper place, of course, for each of the questions we consider in this section: closed, leading, and open. Here we evaluate them from the objective of gaining insight into another's personal story and getting to know them in a deep way.

Closed Questions

The essence of a closed question is that it can be answered with a simple yes or no. There is nothing inherently wrong with closed questions. They are useful when specific information is needed. Nurses must understand a patient's health history, so they will often ask a series of closed questions: "Do you have diabetes? Have any of your relatives had cancer? Are you allergic to any drugs?"

For mentors seeking to get inside the world of their mentees, there are times when closed questions are right and proper. A theater teacher might ask a group of new students: "Have you acted before? Can you sing? Are you feeling a little nervous about being on stage?"

The problem with closed questions is that they seldom reveal the contours and trajectory of a person's story. They center on fulfilling the questioner's desire for particular information but do not result in drawing out the narrative arc of a person's life or her essential characteristics. They result in information about the person, but not the depth of her interior life.

The questioner is in control with closed questions, not the one responding. The parameters are tight: yes or no. As such, closed questions do not provide a context for respondents to truly open up. They might, in fact, put up barriers. A series of closed questions can feel like an interrogation.

Leading Questions

Leading questions suggest or prompt an answer, steering responses in a direction that the questioner believes is valuable or providing a set of answers they believe are correct.

Leading questions are often framed on the heels of statements the questioner makes about his own preferences that suggest the "correct" answer. "Isn't the music at Mass wonderful?" or "I feel such a change of mood in the country after the election, don't you?" or "F. Scott Fitzgerald's novel, *The Great Gatsby,* portrays a moral wasteland. I would not let my younger kids read it. Would you?" are examples of leading questions.

Leading questions are often framed as options assumed to span the full range of possibilities. "Are you a fan of country music, hard rock, soft rock, or classical?" Journalists frequently do this during interviews.

Consider the host on National Public Radio interviewing a soldier about his experiences during the war in Iraq: "Was your decision to enlist as a young man more from a sense of patriotism or more from a sort of boyish desire for adventure?" Leading questions in this vein are problematic because the answers could include all options or none of them, and they often make people feel boxed in. The young man who enlisted could have done so not from patriotism or thirst for adventure but because he needed the money or was led by God or a host of other reasons.

There is a time and a place for leading questions if they are offered with sincere respect and a desire for the good of the other. Parents often need to ask leading questions to effectively guide their children. For example. "Wouldn't you prefer to be at peace with your siblings, rather than in conflict?" "Isn't math fun?" "Will that decision lead to greater conversion of heart or compromise your integrity?"

The problem with leading questions from the standpoint of gaining deep knowledge of the other is that they reflect the mind and opinions of the questioner and often do not succeed in authentically drawing out the respondent's own mind, beliefs, opinions, or feelings.

Open-Ended Questions

Open-ended questions encourage a full, meaningful answer that draws on the subject's knowledge and/or feelings. "Tell me about yourself." "What is your background?" "Why did you come here?"

Such questions invite a deep response. They do not interject the questioner's own beliefs or opinions into the answer. They don't serve up a set of narrow options for the respondent to choose from.

But open-ended questions without context can be too broad and thus confusing. Consider this question posited by Dr. Vincent Hendricks, a professor of logic: "What is the world's most important doctrine?" Doctrine about what? Politics, religion, the economy, or something else? It's *too* open-ended.

The best kinds of open-ended questions provide context,

a basic orientation. They lead, but in a way that invites the person to authentically share. They set the table of a topic without serving the meal. They draw out a free and full response from the other.

Mentors who want to get to know their mentees can and should ask a variety of questions that help their mentees to tell their story. At times, mentors need to ask closed (yes or no) questions. They have their place, but are usually not useful in facilitating authentic sharing. Leading questions are more problematic because through them the questioner tends to impute his own interpretation or agenda into the person's story. Generally, they should be avoided. For the purpose of getting to know the mentee and her story, open-ended questions are much more effective.

THE POWER OF THE ACHIEVEMENT STORY

Open-ended questions that orient mentees to authentically share themselves are definitely the right direction for mentors who want to understand the experience of their mentees. But in this section we are going to further discuss a specific kind of story, the achievement story, (introduced in Chapter Two), which is especially powerful in helping mentees unfold themselves and for mentors to grasp essential features of the mentee's unique personhood.

Consider a scenario where a youth minister, Luca, is trying to get to know a young woman, Maria, in his youth group. "Would you tell me about yourself?" he asks her.

The responses Luca is likely to get with this kind of solid, open-ended question are no doubt valuable for understanding Maria. She might describe her family or place of origin: "I am from Virginia and come from an Irish-Catholic background." Perhaps she shares a bit of her conversion story: "God saved me from drug addiction a year ago and restored my life. It is so good to be back in Church!" She might give her school background: "I'm a student at Lee High School." Or her relationships: "Well, my family and I are very close. I have a steady boyfriend who is really supportive. I'm a dog person and have a little pug named Jasper." Or her major interests: "I am a dancer and love sports. Soccer has been a huge part of my life ever since I was seven years old."

It is certainly true that all of these dimensions of Maria's life are important to her. It is also true that Luca learns about Maria and her story as she shares these aspects of her life. If Luca really wants to learn about Maria, he should ask about those dimensions of her life.

But there is one particular type of open-ended question that allows mentors to quickly and deeply get to know their mentees: the achievement story. It provides an excellent way to get to know others because it helps mentees unveil and share the core aspects of their unique personhood. At the same time, it usually reveals other features of the mentee's life that are a critical part of their life story; for example, their formative relationships or the social and cultural circumstances important to their growth.

"Achievement" does not necessarily mean conformity to contemporary standards of success like a 4.0 GPA or winning awards. It can be about such success, but often it is not. The achievement story is an activity that the person enjoyed doing or had a sense of satisfaction in doing, and believed they did well.

Let's explore a conversation between Luca and Maria oriented by achievement story. Note the questions.

Luca: "Tell me about an activity you've recently done that you deeply enjoyed doing and believe you did well?"

Maria: "Well . . . I love soccer. Last fall I played in a game against our school's archrival, the Blue Devils. I helped our team defeat them and in the final quarter scored the winning goal. That was awesome, especially because I had to overcome a lot to get back on the team."

"What do you love about soccer?"

"I've grown up with it all my life. My dad coached me when I was younger and that was a time when I could be close with him. He and I are both very competitive. We tended to butt heads at home and both have Irish tempers! But he was a great coach and taught me the game. I guess I really like the constant flow of soccer. It's beautiful, but also physical. And I like to win!"

"Tell me about helping to win the game last fall. How did you do that?"

"I played mid-field, my favorite position, and was literally all over the field that day shouting encouragement to the defenders and being a little physical when I had to. One girl kept slamming into my friend Courtney until I slide tackled her in the third quarter and told her to back off. She did after that. But I really liked setting up the forwards to make goals."

"How exactly did you set them up?"

"Something I've always done is pay attention to the whole

field of play. Several times that day I was able to keep the ball for a few seconds while watching the strikers move up field. I anticipated where they were going to get into scoring position and then shot the ball their way. That led to a couple of goals"

"You spoke about having to 'overcome a lot to get back on the team.' What did you mean by that?"

"Well, I have a tendency to live a little on the wild side and a year-and-a-half ago I tried heroin at a party. I had heard that it was addictive, but didn't think it would get me. It did. And in just a couple of months it got so bad I almost died. I had to leave school. My parents gave me tough love and put me in a rehab center. Thank God I met an awesome priest who helped bring me back to the faith. Anyway, I had to fight to get back on the soccer team. I had lost thirty pounds and it took me a while to get strong again."

"What did you do to get back on the team?"

"My coach was suspicious of me at first and I had to regain his trust and the trust of my teammates. I just consistently showed up at practice and worked hard. I prayed a lot! I kept to a good diet. I did not complain, even when my temper flared up. Eventually, I was able to play again."

"What was so satisfying to you about this particular achievement of helping your team beat the Blue Devils?"

"It was the first game I started after getting back on the team. My parents were there in the stands and it was great to have them watch me play so well. But I guess most satisfying was just overcoming. Beating that team. Beating heroin! Finally putting to rest the doubts my teammates and coaches had and regaining their trust."

This conversation in which Maria opens her heart and expresses a story of action that engaged her deeply is framed by three kinds of simple, open-ended questions or prompts.

1. "Tell me about an activity, from any time of life, that you really enjoyed doing and believe you did well." This opens up the mentee to tell his achievement story.

2. "Describe what you actually did." This sort of question takes on different forms depending on a person's initial depiction of what he or she did. It involves follow-up based on the *verbs* mentees use to portray their action. From the example above: "How did you help the team win? How did you get back on the team?" These questions remain open-ended, but naturally connect with the mentee's own narrative.

3. And finally: "What was most satisfying about the achievement activity?" This question is especially powerful, because it draws out specifically what uniquely and intrinsically motivates the mentee.

As Luca draws out Maria's story with sincere empathic interest, he learns a great deal about her. Although the story is about a specific activity, he is able to gain much insight into who she is and critical background which brought her to the youth group. When we clearly see a person share the story of an activity that authentically expresses their unique personhood, they light up and reveal themselves deeply.

It would be premature on the basis of one story to assess Maria as "an overcomer," but it is clear that prevailing over tough obstacles has been a key part of her life. If the same theme continued to show up in Maria's other stories and formed a pattern, then we could highlight "overcoming" as central to Maria.

People do things all day long for all kinds of reasons. People dislike doing certain things but do them anyway in order to conform. They engage in activities because they are compelled to do so out of fear or habit—routine activities that don't really engage the mind or heart.

If we want to understand another—to begin to see her unique nature unfold—it is tremendously powerful to ask open-ended questions about action that deeply engages her. This is exactly what happens in the conversation between Luca and Maria.

It is, of course, true that one achievement story told by the mentee to his or her mentor is not some kind of relational magic that always enables the mentor to plumb the depths of the other, but it is an incredibly powerful way of getting to know him or her—and quickly.

WHAT IF MENTEES DON'T HAVE ANY ACHIEVEMENT STORIES?

In over eighteen years of using this approach in my work, I have never worked with a person who does not have any stories of activities that they enjoyed doing and believed that they did well, even if only moderately so. There are situations, especially among those who have suffered abuse or neglect, where achievement stories can be hard to draw out. Here are some tips for doing so:

First, mentors have to frequently remind people, especially young folks prone to social comparisons, that we are not looking for stories about competitive achievement—being the best, getting the gold star, or being first in class. One's achievements might include these things, but they are not the criteria. Mentees can get stuck on the word "achievement." Help them understand that the term is used broadly. An achievement is any activity that the person enjoyed doing and believed he did well.

Also, be sure to explain that the achievement can be from any sphere of life and any kind of activity. It does not have to be academic or sports-related. It could come from family life, hobbies, private activities, friendships, or anything else. For example, here are some actual achievement stories from high school students in my *Discerning Personal Vocation* course:

> *Tess*: "When I got my dog, I took the responsibility of training him. I taught him the play position, climb, jump, over, under, bark, and head down. But I did not stop there, I wanted to teach him hand signals. Now, he knows these commands without me ever saying a word."

> *Luke*: "Because of continued and faithful service to our local parish I was invited to become a 'Pon-

tifical Server' to assist our local Bishop at special Masses and services. This has been an honor and a pleasure for me."

Clare: "My sisters and I wrote and produced my own personal album for my dad's birthday."

John: "I coached my little brothers' U8 Soccer team two years in a row. The second year we had a kid on the team with some serious behavioral issues, but I managed to deal with him and still coach the rest of the team for three months."

If a person still has trouble coming up with stories at this point, you can simply ask, "What kinds of things do you like to do?" With this question, you pull attention away from the person did *well*. Simply help him draw stories from a list of things that he just likes doing. Often, as people start to talk about these actions they will recognize achievement in them or at least be drawn into positive memory of action that is truly expressive of their unique nature.

THE GOOD FRUIT OF DRAWING OUT ACHIEVEMENT STORIES

Several benefits emerge from mentors drawing out the achievement stories of their mentees.

First, those sharing are engaged in memories of action that was full of joy and authentic fulfillment. In recollecting these memories, they re-present them and have the opportunity, at least in part, to relive them. What a gift!

Second, because the achievement story is about what the person did well and enjoyed doing it is often about his unique strengths. Thus, it can be incredibly positive and affirming.

Third, the very process of people recollecting their achievement stories can cultivate much deeper self-awareness. Seldom are people asked to share their achievement stories. And when they are asked the broad question, "Tell me about yourself," they usually don't choose to unfold achievement stories. Those who have not taken the time to consider their stories won't effectively discern their own unique gifts, which is a key aspect of vocational discernment.

Fourth, this process involves attentive and empathic listening, which is an act of great love for the mentee. It's a love oriented toward the flourishing of the person, a love which desires that the other be revealed according to God's design and fulfill that design.

On the inscapevocations.com site, we share information about MCORE, a narrative-based online assessment that mentors and mentees can take to identify their core motivations. MCORE is based upon three achievement stories and results in a robust report that helps people gain insight into their unique motivational design and its implications for living life well.

EMPATHIC LISTENING

"But when someone understands how it feels and
seems to be ME, without wanting to analyze me
or judge me, then I can blossom and grow in that
climate. And research bears out this common
observation. When the therapist can grasp the
moment-to-moment experiencing which occurs
in the inner world of the client as the client sees it
and feels it, without losing the separateness of his
own identity in this empathic process, then change
is likely to occur."

—CARL ROGERS—

*On Becoming a Person:
A Therapist's View of Psychotherapy*

Approaching mentees with open-ended questions that
express sincere interest in their lives is a powerful way
for mentors to transcend themselves, the first movement
of empathy. Such questions imply that mentors will actually make space in their own interior life and truly listen.
Empathic listening is difficult. In this section we draw from
Steven Covey, celebrated author of *Seven Habits of Highly
Effective People*, on how to do it well.

Far more important than technique is a basic disposition of empathy. But if one has the right disposition yet lacks
polished technique, he will still be much better off. There
are three fundamental elements to a disposition of empathy.

First, a mentor must truly love the mentee. This can't be
taken for granted. Loving him involves constantly holding

in mind and heart the intention that each mentee become who he is created to be. Christ's love is keenly focused on each person so that he might flourish. This is the ultimate example for mentors. "Love each other as God loves each one of you," said Mother Teresa, "with an intense and particular love."

Second, one's disposition should not be closed or guarded, but open and actively receptive. Here body language is important. A furrowed brow and crossed arms are much less likely to draw out authentic response than warm eyes and an open, disarming physical stance. The interior of the mentor should be one of quiet waiting and not restless anticipation to press a point or make a case.

Third, the mentor should have a sincere desire to understand the mentee. As Stephen Covey says, "If you really seek to understand, without hypocrisy and guile, there will be times when you will be literally stunned with the pure knowledge and understanding that will flow to you from another human being."[1] In this stance one's own agenda is pushed to the periphery of consciousness and space is created for listening to the other.

If you have these three dispositions down—loving intention that the person becomes who they are created to be, openness to the other, sincere desire to understand—the kind of technique we are about to discuss will flow easily.

The right method is important since through it one can develop habits of empathy. If one is still learning technique

---

[1] Stephen Covey, *Seven Habits of Highly Effective People* (New York: Simon & Schuster, 1990), 252.

but holds the basic dispositions, the errors in technique will not interfere much in the process—especially if the mentor actively works to become more empathic.

BASIC ELEMENTS OF EMPATHIC LISTENING

Mentors should be attentive to mentees using both sides of their brains. The left side is more reason-focused—the logical side of the brain. The right side of the brain is responsible for visual, intuitive, and more feeling-focused modes of perception. It is impossible to listen empathically on the basis of words alone.

Consider the scenario of a family with a bunch of cats. The wife and kids simply adore cats and seem to always be open to getting another one, but Dad can't stand the sight of them.

We find husband and wife together at the top of the driveway raking the fall leaves. Up comes the neighbor, Jenny, in her Chevrolet S-10 pick-up truck with a stray cat, knowing that the family often takes them. She comes to a stop and asks enthusiastically: "Would you like another cat? I just found this stray." Now listen with both sides of your brain to the response from husband and wife.

Mom, with smiling eager eyes, rushes to the truck, and declares: "I would be so happy to take another cat!"

Dad, with stiff posture, tight jaw, hand gripped on rake, and icy tone, says: "I would be so happy to take another . . . cat!"

Mom and Dad use the same phrase but obviously express very different meanings. One is sincerely open to the cat. The other, who is clearly being facetious, is definitely not. Deep listening requires much more than understanding the logical meaning of words. Tone, body language, and expression of the eyes must all be perceived carefully to truly understand another person.

When mentors use both the left (logical) and right (feeling) sides of their brains, the two-part technique that we discuss below can be activated. Empathic listening requires the mentor to reflect back both content and feeling to the one speaking. To reflect the words spoken, mentors ought not simply repeat what they hear. This can sound like parroting or mimicking and have the effect of irritating speakers, rather than drawing them out. Exact repetition can also sound gimmicky and give the impression that the mentor has an agenda beyond really listening.

When reflecting content, the mentor should summarize *in her own words* what she heard without changing the meaning of what the mentee spoke. There are several good reasons for this kind of reflection. First, when the mentor summarizes using her own words she is forced to truly understand what is said. Second, she gives clear evidence to the mentee that she has been heard. Third, it is almost always advantageous to the mentee that her words are reflected. We need physical mirrors to recognize how we present ourselves to the world and make adjustments when they reflect tousled hair or dirt smears on our cheeks. Similarly, mentees whose words have been brash, unclear, or problematic in some way make positive adjustments to what they have said when they hear it spoken back to them.

While summarizing verbal content, the mentor should reflect in tone and body language the emotion of the mentee. Again, this should not be strictly imitative but done in a way that acknowledges the feelings of the mentee. If verbal content is reflected without corresponding emotional content, the mentor can seem cold and unmoved.

How about when the mentee's emotions are wildly out of control or barely registering a pulse? While it would be imprudent for mentors to reflect those emotions at the level they are displayed, it is valuable for them to reach emotively in the direction of the mentee's feelings and share in them at some level. This could mean that a mentor raises his tempo and volume when speaking to a mentee whose emotions are high, or that a mentor adopts a quiet and more subdued tone for a mentee who is feeling low. Without the mentor offering some similar level of emotional reflection, a chasm will appear in the conversation. As Scripture says, "He who sings songs to a heavy heart is like one who takes off a garment on a cold day, and like vinegar on a wound" (Prov 25:20).

Consider now two versions of a conversation between a mother and her eighteen-year-old son, Judah, who is a senior in high school and considering enlisting in the Marine Corps. The mother expresses love for her son in both versions but notice to what extent she practices empathy in each.

Judah (cautiously, quietly): "Mom, I've been thinking lately about the Marine Corps. As you know, I had been planning to go to college right away but . . . I might want to enlist in the Marines right after high school."

Mom (eyes widening, loudly): "What? When did this happen?

"Well, a few weeks ago at the school career fair I met a sergeant who told me the Marine Corps story. It really interested me. The Marines are always first in battle. They are America's elite fighting force."

"Judah, do really think you can kill a human being? Because that's what you'll be trained to do."

"Well, I wouldn't want to, Mom, but if I had to defend my country, I would."

"Did the sergeant tell you about Post-Traumatic Stress Disorder and how it ruins soldiers' lives?"

"No (defensively, voice raising), but he did say being a Marine was tough and not for the fainthearted."

"Tough and hardened. Oh, Judah! I can't stand the thought of you going into the Marine Corps. I know that we need the armed forces to defend our country, but look at what happens to young men who come out of the service. Do you remember Daniel from your youth group?

"Yeah! I still see him and we've talked about his experience in the Marines. He went to Afghanistan. He said it was hard but that he learned—"

"The first thing Daniel did after enlisting was put himself in debt with a new Camaro—and he started smoking!

"I'm not going to start smoking, Mom!"

"But, Judah, there are certain things that you would have to do as a Marine. You would be under government authority. And what if you were asked to do something that violated your conscience? The way our country is going—"

"Let's just stop talking about it, Mom."

In this first scenario we see a mother interested in her son's well-being. She wants what she believes is best for him, but her questions come from a place of fear and her comments are all about persuading Judah not to go through with his plans. She shows little regard for her son's perspective or for helping him to discern what he ought to do. A conversation that could have led the mother to know her son better, to help him grow in self-awareness, and to cultivate his own calling ends abruptly and fruitlessly.

In the second version of the conversation pay attention to the mother's empathy as she asks questions and listens.

Judah (cautiously, quietly): "Mom, I've been thinking lately about the Marine Corps. As you know I had been planning to go to college right away but . . . I might want to enlist in the Marines right after high school."

Mom (slowly, quietly): "You've had a shift in your thinking about what to do after high school. That's not uncommon, Judah. What interests you in the Marine Corps?"

"Well, a few weeks ago at the school career fair I met a sergeant who told me the Marine Corps' story. It really interested me. The Marines are always first in battle. They are America's finest fighting force. Once a Marine, always a Marine. I would be able to serve my country at a time of need! I would learn a lot about leadership and teamwork. And, after four years, I would have a really good scholarship for college."

"The Marine Corps is an elite, dedicated group of men. You believe you might be able to serve your country well if you were to join. You are seeing other opportunities too: life *lessons, money for college. What have you done to decide if you should enlist?"*

"Well, I'm seeing a lot of positives. Just spoke to the sergeant a couple of weeks ago. I've not really thought of any negatives. I'm sure there are some."

Mom (gently smiling): "You are seeing a lot of advantages to joining the Marine Corps, but not yet the disadvantages. What could those be?"

Judah (voice slowing down, brow furrowing): "Well— having to go to war and kill somebody or get killed."

"Taking the life of another human being and putting your own life on the line are serious matters. Have you prayed about this decision?"

"Not yet, Mom, but I know I need to do that. And I will."

In the second conversation, Judah's mom is a picture of the empathic mentor. She summarizes what he says and reflects his feelings. She lets him know that she understands, which invites him to share authentically. She asks open-ended questions that acknowledge his interest in the Marine Corps but also help him grow in self-awareness and effectively discern. The conversation ends with Judah wanting to think more carefully and take the time to pray.

Earlier, we discussed several benefits for mentees and the mentor relationship that emerge from drawing out achievement stories through empathic inquiry. There are at least two profound benefits to this relationship when mentors listen with empathy.

First, people long to be understood and affirmed for being the *unique good* that they are. After physical survival, this is the greatest human need. Mentors have the opportunity to meet it on a regular basis through empathic listening which wordlessly but clearly declares to mentees: "You are good. You are loved. You have profound value and dignity because you exist."

A second benefit follows from the first. Empathic listening is the necessary precursor to direct influence. It shows that mentors care and have taken into consideration the needs, concerns, and questions of the mentees. When mentees are affirmed and confident they are understood, they open the door for learning and growing.

Pope Francis has spoken beautifully about the "the loving look," the look Jesus gives when He silently but powerfully declares particular love to an unrepeatable person. Through empathic inquiry and listening, mentors offer this kind of loving look to the youth under their care. It is a look that helps to cast out anxiety born from fear of judgment. Under the loving gaze of a mentor, a young person can take the risks that only love takes—that he *must* take—in order to live in the true freedom of the sons of God.

5

A CULTURE OF VOCATION

Luke Burgis

"It is time now for us to rise from sleep."

—ST. BENEDICT OF NURSIA—

The Rule of St. Benedict

IN THE summer of 2013, I was sent to the small, lakeside town of Verbania in northern Italy to try to learn Italian in six weeks before starting theology classes (which would be taught in Italian) in Rome. I thought I had a bright idea. I went to a bookshop and bought a copy of *Pinocchio* in the original Italian. Reading a children's book would be a good way to start learning the language, I thought, and it might be fun. When I showed it to my tutor the next day, she laughed at me. "*Pinocchio* isn't a children's book!" she said.

The Disney movie had duped me. Critics treat it as a simple morality tale that teaches children the benefits of hard work and middle-class values like honesty, bravery, and sacrifice. That's about as naïve as Pinocchio himself. Carlo Collodi, the author, wrote the book in the throes of the Industrial Revolution during the unification of

Italy and the rise of socialist and authoritarian systems in Europe and Russia.

Pinocchio is the story of a marionette. What's a marionette? It's a puppet controlled by strings attached to its limbs, and its movements are determined entirely by the forces acting upon it.

But Pinocchio is a peculiar kind of marionette. After a miraculous event, he no longer has strings attached to him. He's able to make *choices* that determine whether or not he will become a "real boy." He is in a perilous situation, though, because he lives in a world where most of the characters he meets are manipulative. They use him to satisfy their own desires.

Fortunately, Pinocchio has a few friends who help him along the way. In the end, they are able to help Pinocchio overcome the forces that threaten to thwart his vocation, and he achieves his dream of becoming a "real boy" who is able to think and act in freedom.

So make some popcorn and pour yourself a drink. *Pinocchio* reveals all five of the core elements that any "culture of vocation" must include: personal encounter, true language, wonder, creativity, and incarnation (or a preference for flesh over wood).

First, *personal encounter*. In the film, Pinocchio encounters a variety of characters that influence him. Some of them—Geppetto, the Blue Fairy, and Jiminy Cricket—know and care about what is good for him. Almost all of the other characters want to exploit him.

In the beginning, his benevolent creator and father, Geppetto, wishes upon a star that Pinocchio might become a real boy. This is symbolic for giving a transcendent purpose to his existence. Pinocchio is then granted the gift of life by the Blue Fairy.

That's just a start, though. Whether or not he becomes a real boy depends on the choices he makes. He can become a real boy by doing the "good" and rejecting the "bad"—but it's not always clear what's good and what's bad. There are many competing forces in Pinocchio's life. Each encounter helps him move closer to or further away from becoming a real boy.

In the *personal encounter* section of this chapter, we discuss the critical role that each of us plays in helping others discover, embrace, and live out their callings. Building a culture of vocation starts with personal and ongoing conversion, prayer, and a commitment to living our own calling.

Second, *language*. Pinocchio's journey depends upon whether or not he tells the truth. Each person's vocational discernment depends on speaking and living in the truth. When we lie, our nose does not necessarily grow longer. We are, however, torn apart and divided against ourselves. At a young age, children can feel a lie in their gut (this is a well-documented physiological reality). Their conscience has not yet been confused by self-deception.

To build a culture of vocation, we have to re-examine the type of language that we use. We can't stir stale water. We should speak words of life—words that are fresh, true, and edifying—in a language that others can understand. If we model how to always speak the truth in love, others may find the courage to do the same.

The final three elements of a culture of vocation correspond to the three anti-vocational phenomena discussed in chapter one.

Wonder. In response to a culture of calculation we can foster a culture of wonder. Every character that Pinocchio encounters makes him an object of calculation to satisfy his business interests. None of them stand before him in wonder (he's a marionette that moves without strings, for heaven's sake!) more than five seconds before selling him into their system. Wonder is the antidote to calculation because it allows us to be surprised. If God wonders at us ("What is man that you are mindful of him, and the son of man that you care for him?" wonders the psalmist in 8:4), then how much more should we wonder at even the most seemingly uninteresting person that we meet today?

Incarnation. In response to a culture of disincarnation we must live the Incarnation of Christ, which was not only a one-time historical event, but brought about the transformation of the cosmos. The Word became flesh. God's *Logos* became one with us down to the cellular level. Pinocchio's vocation is to become a real boy with real flesh and bones. This is what God wants for every person. "A new heart I will give you, and a new spirit I will put within you; and I will take out of your flesh the heart of stone and give you a heart of flesh," speaks the prophet Ezekiel (36:26). We will not build a culture of vocation by proposing high-minded ideas but by living out our vocations in hot-blooded bodies that can touch, feel, see, hear, and taste the reality of God and proclaim the Gospel through them.

Lastly, *creativity.* In response to a culture of conformity we must develop a culture of creativity that helps each person live in creative fidelity to the truth rather than the puppeteers of modern society. Anyone with enough training and discipline can follow external commands. Even a well-trained dog can do that.

The funeral oration of Pericles contrasts the Athenians to the Spartans: while the Spartans become skilled warriors through a rigid system of training (*askesis*) and external laws mandating combat, the Athenians are more praiseworthy because they have learned to follow the impulse of inward character and freely perform great actions that the Spartans do out of compulsion.[1] In any culture of vocation, we must honor the free, creative expression of every person in discovering his own particular way of conforming to the Truth.

All five of these core elements of a vocational culture start with education. In the film *Pinocchio*, Geppetto rushes Pinocchio off to school with an apple for his teacher and a book in his hand. "You've got to go to school to learn things and get smart," he says. When Pinocchio asks why, Geppetto responds: "Because!"

This is when Pinocchio's troubles begin. No sooner does he turn the corner to go to school than the conniving fox notices him and co-opts his education by whisking him off with promises of fame.

Pinocchio deserved a better answer to the question, "Why school?" Millions of young people are asking the same question today. If we can't answer the question—if we can't help the next generation of students go into the world with a sense of purpose and the ability to discern what is good—

---

[1] See Thucydides' *History of the Peloponnesian War.*

there are plenty of other people who will. And they may not always be friendly.

EDUCATION

"What matters school? We can go to school tomorrow. Whether we have a lesson more or a lesson less, we shall always remain the same donkeys."

—CARLO COLLODI—

Pinocchio

Brand name colleges extract enormous rents for their imprimatur, but their promises (enlightenment, maturity, life-long stability) are no longer worthy of belief. Yet these institutions market themselves as a necessary rite of passage even while students are graduating with record levels of debt, lacking direction, and facing total uncertainty about the future.

Students are graduating with record levels of debt, lacking direction and facing total uncertainty about the future. Without purpose, students are co-opted into the postmodern belief that everything is open to an infinite number of interpretations. They focus on degree requirements, social life, and a hodgepodge of social justice issues. They lack a transcendent purpose that gives unity and meaning to their lives.

Before long, students are disillusioned (the perils of being a puppet are legion), and a savior comes along with an easy way out. For Pinocchio, it was his "friend," the Fox. He convinces Pinocchio that he's a victim who needs a vacation rather than someone who needs to take responsibility for his life. The Fox offers Pinocchio a trip to Pleasure Island, where instant gratification reigns. "Right here, boys!" they hear upon arrival. "Get your cake, pie, dill pickles, and ice cream! Stuff yourselves! It's all free, boys! It's all free! Hurry, hurry, hurry, hurry!" By the end of the night, Pinocchio is chomping on a cigar and shooting pool with his new friends.

But remember what happens on Pleasure Island: children become braying donkeys in a totalitarian system that turns them, literally, into jackasses. They can no longer think or speak for themselves. They lose their personalities, and they lose all sense of purpose.

Pinocchio barely escapes before his transformation is complete.

This is not a children's story. This is the state of modern education.

The good news is that there's a purpose of education that transcends the limited bounds of campus, the margins of a resume, and the shores of Pleasure Island—one that transforms students into responsible citizens, and sometimes even saints, instead of jackasses.

The concept of *paideia*, the education of citizens in the integral good of the human person, was central to Greek culture 2,500 years ago. The entire Greek community took responsibility for shaping the values of its young citizens so that they could achieve excellence in every area of their lives. Christianity transformed *paideia* by rooting the formation of human persons not in the image of the ideal citizen (as in the Greek *polis*, or city), but in the image of Jesus Christ, *perfectus deus, perfectus homo*, who "*reveals man to himself* and brings to light his most high calling" (RH §8).

Archbishop Charles Chaput wrote that the goal of education in the Archdiocese of Philadelphia is to "equip saints for life in this world and the next." Even education in its secular form—education that does not proclaim Jesus as the Way, the Truth, and the Life—should at least form students who are capable of discovering the reality of Christian faith rather than obscuring, confusing, or becoming a scandal (from *skandalon*, literally a "stumbling block") to religious belief. In other words, all education should form people who can be saints.

In his book *Prayer as a Political Problem*, Jean Danielou, S.J., wrote, "If politics does not create conditions in which man can completely fulfill himself, it becomes an impediment to that fulfillment."[2] We can substitute "education" for "politics" and arrive at the same conclusion.

Education should give students the ability to navigate the hostile world that we live in—one not unlike Pinocchio's—so as to live in the true freedom that will allow them to fulfill their vocations. It should form people *capable of discernment* who can discern "whatever is true, whatever is honorable, whatever is just, whatever is pure, whatever is lovely, whatever is gracious" (Phil 4:8).

This can be done without an explicit focus on theological formation because there are always *semina Verbi*, seeds of the Word, which can be cultivated through personal encounter, language, wonder, incarnation, and creativity.

In the 1970s, Dr. John Senior and his colleagues at the University of Kansas launched the Integrated Humanities

---

2 Jean Daniélou, *L'Oraison problème politique* (Bibliothèque du Cerf, 2012), 26.

Program which was designed to instill wonder and foster the pursuit of truth in undergraduate students. They stargazed, recited poetry, and read the books that shaped Western civilization. So many students had conversion experiences and embraced their vocations (including many as priests and religious) that the program eventually came under suspicion by the university's leadership and was shut down.

The Integrated Humanities Program did not explicitly champion Christianity, but students were led to Christ by their passionate pursuit of the truth. It was an authentic humanities program because it exposed students to all that is truly human, including the most human thing of all: wonder in front of the numinous, the *mysterium fascinans et tremendum* (the mystery that both fascinates and makes one tremble) that permeates our existence. The program opened the door to saintliness because it formed students with a spirit of discernment, capable of wonder, woken from the slumber of mediocrity that is learned in a world that tells us that the highest aim of our existence is to be a "good person" (which, according to our secular world, means you haven't killed anybody, you pay your taxes, and you never make anyone feel bad).

There are reasons to believe that a more intentional exploration of vocation will benefit college students, too. In 1999, the Lilly Endowment undertook a project to see what would happen if a culture of vocation was woven into the undergraduate experience in a variety of church-affiliated colleges and universities. The schools were diverse, from acclaimed research universities to small liberal arts colleges, and they had a wide range of religious commitment.

Eighty-eight schools were selected from over four hundred applicants. Over $225 million in grant money was awarded in order to implement the Program for the Theological Exploration of Vocation (PTEV). Each of the participating colleges implemented new curriculum, seminars, mentoring relationships, and other support for students to explore vocation within their unique institutional contexts. They regularly engaged the fundamental questions "So what?" and "Who cares?" The results were extraordinary.

Tim Clydesdale, author of *The Purposeful Graduate: Why Colleges Must Talk to Students about Vocation*, interviewed hundreds of recent college graduates to try to understand the effects of the PTEV. He tells story after story of students and institutions that benefited from an organizational focus on helping students understand their lives as a vocation. Those who participated in PTEV expressed broader satisfaction with life after college than did those who did not across six key categories: work or graduate school life, finances, living arrangements, social life, love life, and spiritual life.[3]

Of the eighty-eight participating schools, eighty-three campuses chose to continue their programs in some form after the initial grant period. Eighty-six percent of faculty respondents agreed or strongly agreed that their campus's exploration programs had "positively impacted my own work"; seventy-five percent agreed that participation "helped me hone my own sense of 'vocation,' 'calling,' or

---

[3] A statistically significant result that held firm even after controlling for respondents' gender, race, age, socioeconomic status, and attendance at religious services.

'purpose,'" and eighty-five percent said that participation "deepened my appreciation for the mission of [this school]." The percentages were even higher among staff participants— ninety percent, eighty-four percent, and ninety-three percent, respectively. Clydesdale's key takeaway was that "purpose exploration produces a pattern of examined living and positive engagement with others, thereby increasing the odds that emerging adults will flourish after they graduate from college."[4]

A vocational culture in education is what John Henry Newman essentially articulated in his lectures, *The Idea of a University*. The purpose of a university begins and ends with the purpose of its students, and each of them was made for heaven. All of the knowledge in the world is not enough to make good citizens, let alone saints. "Quarry rock with razors, or moor a vessel with a thread of silk," he wrote, "then may you hope with such keen and delicate instruments as human knowledge and human reason to contend against those giants, the passion and pride of man."[5]

According to Newman, the will is not engaged by ideas but by personalities, and institutions have personalities. An education is not simply a collection of classes, clubs, and core requirements—it's a culture. So important was the culture of a university to Newman that he preferred a vibrant, student-led Oxford with empty classrooms and no

---

[4] Timothy Clydesdale, *The Purposeful Graduate: Why Colleges Must Talk to Students about Vocation* (Chicago: University of Chicago Press, 2015), 124.

[5] John Henry Newman, *Discourses on the Scope and Nature of University Education: Addressed to the Catholics of Dublin* (Cambridge: Cambridge University Press, 2010), 196.

professors to a culturally dead Oxford where stuffy professors designed curriculum for disembodied, interchangeable students.

A university is a living organism, and it should be full of life. Give Newman a fiery, fist-pounding debate between classmates over the meaning of "just war theory" settled by a wrestling match in the quad over a professor whose only wrestling is morning bouts with bow ties. Newman thought that integral human development happens when the entire person is engaged. It's better to make students laugh, cry, and get upset than to have a culture so sterile that it provokes no human response.

For Thomas Aquinas, integral human development is rooted in love. A person might have a penetrating intellect, athletic prowess, or an inclination to serve others, but these things only make him "good" in one way. Since the will governs all of the other faculties—and what makes the will "good" is love—it is love alone that is capable of making a person good. It is the form of every virtue and the force that directs the pursuit of knowledge.

Education is about learning how to love, and love is the business of saints. A saint, after all, is a person who has learned to love in love's highest and fullest expression.

All five elements of a vocational culture are rooted in love and lead to love. Love is personal, it is expressed in language, it wonders, it is incarnate, and it is creative. Most importantly, it is active. Love *does*.

THE FIVE ELEMENTS OF A VOCATIONAL CULTURE

At a conference on vocations in January 2017, Pope Francis said that there is an urgency to bring forth a new "vocational culture" in the Church.[6] He encouraged the faithful to find courageous new ways to announce the Gospel of vocation. To describe what a vocation is like, he used the image of a spring of water hidden deep in the earth that waits for the right moment to gush forth. In our deserts of vocation, there are millions of springs waiting to burst forth and spread life-giving water to the rest of the land.

People are thirsty. The five elements of a vocational culture that follow are about *knowing* and *loving* each person in our lives so that the spring of water within them can flow freely. It starts with an encounter.

Personal Encounter

We won't build a culture of vocation by handing out educational pamphlets, making presentations, organizing conferences, or getting better at using social media. Living movements don't come by committee, and propositions don't change hearts. But "persons influence us, voices melt us, looks subdue us, deeds inflame us," wrote Cardinal John Henry Newman.[7]

---

[6] Pope Francis, Address at convention of the Italian Bishops' Conference Office of Vocation titled "Rise, go and do not fear. Vocation and Holiness: I am on a mission" (January 5, 2017).

[7] John Henry Newman, *An Essay in Aid of a Grammar of Assent* (New York: The Catholic Publication Society, 1870), 89–90.

We have to risk complicating our lives, fleeing the neat confines of self in order to go out to the other and meet him in an unknown territory on the periphery. This is how we encounter people as mysteries and not problems. To treat a person as a problem is to keep him at a safe distance. But to look at him as a mystery—and every person is a mystery—is to *get involved in his life,* to become a full participant.

Personal encounters are critical because the most common means to reveal and transmit the truth isn't books or formulas—it's people. History has born this out. Eleven of the twelve Apostles were martyred for the truth of what they had seen and heard. Since then, about seventy million Christians have given their lives for that same truth. It's estimated that in the past decade alone, nine hundred thousand Christians have been martyred for their faith.[8] Imagine instead if they had proclaimed Christ in word alone, without the testimony of their lives. The world would be a very different place. So it is with our vocations.

On a damp chilly spring day in 2017, I took the train from Grand Central Station to Tarrytown, New York, to the Stone Barns Center for Food & Agriculture and spent an afternoon with Fred Kirschenmann, the President of the Board of Stone Barns. I'd read his essay, "Theological Reflections while Castrating a Calf," and wanted to know how to have theological reflections while castrating a calf (first I'd have to learn how to castrate a calf).

---

[8] The Center for the Study of Global Christianity, citing the following study: http://www.gordonconwell.edu/ockenga/research/documents/2Countingmartyrsmethodology.pdf

I learned that Fred's life changed with an encounter. He earned his doctorate in philosophy from the University of Chicago and became director of the Consortium for Higher Education Religion Studies in Dayton, Ohio in the early seventies. There he met a student, David Vetter, who changed his life. "I was immediately drawn to him," says Fred, because he was one of the first people talking about the importance of caring for the soil.

David had been researching the impact of organic field management on soil quality, and he was passionate about developing a land ethic that could be put into practice on a real farm. When Fred's father had a heart attack, Fred decided to leave academia and return home to his family's farm in North Dakota. Inspired by his friendship with David, Fred converted his family's three-thousand-acre grain and livestock operation into an organic farm.

A chance encounter with a student gave a new trajectory to Fred's life. Today, he is one of the leading voices in ecology. His eighteen-hundred-acre organic farm was profiled in the award-winning film, *My Father's Garden*, and he won the Lifetime Achievement Award from the International Federation of Organic Agriculture Movements in 2014.

I asked Fred what it was like to leave a tenure-track academic career and move back to the family farm. "I've never done anything that I've planned," he said. "I've only responded to stuff that comes up."

Fred responded to his father, and it gave his entire life a new meaning. Fred told me that his father grew up in the Dust Bowl in the 1930s. "My father was an incredibly thoughtful person of deep insights. . . . He knew somehow that the dustbowl wasn't just about the weather, which most of his neighbors thought. It was also about the way farmers farmed." He knew the Dust Bowl far beyond the limits of his sixth grade education. He had tacit knowledge.

"He became a radical advocate of the importance of taking care of the land," Fred said. "I can still see him in my mind's eye lecturing me with his finger stuck out at me, telling me how important it was to take care of the land." He passed those insights down to his son, Fred, who never forgot the way that he looked when he pointed his finger.

And as we walked around the farm that day, I could tell that Fred, like his father, knew the land in a way that one could never know by reading about it in books. He knew it by connaturality. He knew it because he had dwelt on it all of his life.

A child learns trust by looking into his father's eyes during a thunderstorm. We learn about the reality of personal calling by watching a farmer walk his land, a master craftsman at his craft, a mother nursing her child. Their actions reveal truths that words fail to capture.

The Apostles learned who Jesus was in this way. "But there are also many other things which Jesus did; were every one of them to be written, I suppose that the world itself could not contain the books that would be written" (John 21:25).

They discovered their vocations through a personal encounter.

Language

Shortly after Geppetto discovers Pinocchio alive, he introduces him to the cat, Figaro. "Say hello to Figaro!" he tells Pinocchio. "Hello to Figaro!" echoes Pinocchio.

He can't distinguish the command ("Say") from the content ("Hello") from the object ("Figaro"). He isn't fully human at this point in the story, so he can only repeat what he hears—words without meaning. He hasn't had much contact with reality yet, so his words are empty.

C. S. Lewis understood the difference between words and meaning. "Reason is the natural organ of truth: but imagination is the organ of meaning," he wrote in his essay "Bluspels and Flalansferes." Lewis believed that we don't truly grasp the meaning of any word or concept until we have a clear picture or image connected to it. He likens the fickleness of human desire to one who prefers to make mud pies in a slum to a holiday at the sea because he cannot yet imagine what a holiday at the sea is like.

Perhaps this is a problem in the work of cultivating vocations, too. Can young people really imagine what a "vocation well lived" is? Do they have an image of what that looks that?

In one of his best-known Anglican sermons, "Unreal Words," John Henry Newman exhorts Christians not to say words or phrases that trivialize the profound realities they are referring to. He wanted people to fully realize the truths that they were professing so nonchalantly. In his sermon, he warns against the mode in which people speak of the shortness and vanity of life, the certainty of death, the joys of heaven. They have commonplaces in their mouths . . . making remarks true and sound, and in themselves deep, yet *unmeaning in their mouths*. . . . Or when they fall into sin, they speak of man being frail, of the deceitfulness of the human heart, of God's mercy, and so on—all these great words, heaven, hell, judgment, mercy, repentance, works, the world that now is, the world to come, being little more than "lifeless sounds" . . . in their mouths and ears . . . as the proprieties of conversation, or the civilities of good breeding.[9]

We should check ourselves. The word "vocation" itself is often used in an equivocal way—to refer to the vocation of every person one moment, and the vocation of only priests and religious the next. To make matters even more confusing, "vocational training" is commonly understood to mean learning a trade or marketable skill—plumbing, electrical work, or construction—in preparation for employment. With so much clutter around the word "vocation," we have to make an intentional effort to recover its theological meaning and the full force of its implications.

We also hear about some people "having" a vocation. In what sense does one "have" a vocation? A vocation is a call from God—a complete gift—that can only be received in

---

[9] John Henry Newman, *Realizations: Newman's Own Selection of His Sermons*, ed. Vincent Ferrer Blehl (Collegeville: Liturgical Press, 2009), 78.

gratitude and responded to through the gift of one's life. A vocation is on the level of *being*, not on the level of *having*. Everybody is being called, but not everybody is responding.

If we're going to create a culture of vocation, we have to speak in a language that doesn't betray it.

When I first entered seminary formation, I spoke to a priest who told me the story of one seminarian from our diocese who "unfortunately didn't persevere." The word "persevere" stuck in my head. I later learned that this particular seminarian discerned, quite confidently, that he was not called to the priesthood.

There's nothing noble about persevering on the wrong path simply for the sake of persevering. Yet that type of language appealed to the shadow-side of my motivational drive. *I am one who perseveres*, I thought. The idea that I might not persevere terrified me. At the time, I didn't have the spiritual maturity to put the priest's well-intentioned encouragement in proper context.

Often, young men and women discerning a vocation—any vocation—are very sensitive to the opinions of others. We have to be mindful of this and give them space to discern God's will, not ours.

John Henry Newman's "Unreal Words" is a call to take words seriously. When we say things that we don't really mean—when we parrot clichés or say things that we think other people want to hear, when we conform our language to the sanitized, popular aphorisms within a community—we begin to be divided against ourselves.

Living in a seminary with two hundred and fifty other men for a time was a study in authenticity for me. During the first six months after our arrival in Rome, everyone was "good"—all day every day (even when we chatted at six in the morning on the way to the chapel). Even if a guy was seriously doubting whether or not he was supposed to be there, he would say things like "God-willing, I'll be ordained next year." Five days later, he would be gone. Over time, the veneer gave way to the occasional, "Man, I'm tired and stressed!" And what a sweet sound that was.

Here are important habits of discernment related to language: try never to say anything unreal, stop lying (consciously or unconsciously), and develop a dogged commitment to speaking authentically in every situation. The truth burns, and it will burn away all of the falsity that contaminates discernment.

Jordan Peterson, a psychology professor at the University of Toronto, advises his students to think carefully about how much of what they say is not an authentic expression of who they are. He recommends something like a "particular examination of conscience" at the end of every day. When Peterson first started the practice, he was mortified to find that about ninety-five percent of everything he said was false. The falsehoods had to be burned away like the dead wood in a forest so he could begin to speak fruitfully and powerfully about the things that truly mattered to him.

If the task seems daunting, we can take a page out of Ernest Hemmingway's book. When he was struggling with writer's block, he had a simple rule: write one true sentence. And after that, write another one. And another.

Sometimes, the truth burns. But it always liberates.

A Culture of Wonder: The Antidote to a Culture of Calculation

> "Men go abroad to wonder at the heights of mountains, at the huge waves of the sea, at the long courses of the rivers, at the vast compass of the ocean, at the circular motions of the stars, and they pass by themselves without wondering."
>
> —ST. AUGUSTINE—
> *Confessions*

Nineteenth century Parisian *flâneurs*—men and woman of leisure whom Honoré de Balzac described as practicing "the gastronomy of the eye"—were known to bring pet turtles with them on their strolls through the parks to help them slow their pace and feast on the wonders around them.

Today, they'd be turtle soup.

Our culture of calculation moves fast. Google sifts through about two hundred million search results in less than half a second. The company admits that its entire strategy is "to get users in and out really quickly"—the faster that people move through information, the more money Google makes. If we take the time to dwell in something, we're not searching.

We program computers, and then our computers program us. We've learned to search for and discard millions of options every day. All of Google's algorithms are built on cold calculations about what might be valuable to us.

These calculations result in a throwaway culture as boring as the numbers that it's built on. When is the last time that you wondered in amazement at a search result?

A vocation is lived by a person who arrives at an unrepeatable result: a unique relationship with God for all eternity. It is shot through and through with events that surpass our ability to understand them in this life—a chance run-in, an open door, an unexpected turn. A vocation is traveled in wonder, known in faith.

How can we not wonder at life? One way is to make it the object of calculation. Consider the mystery of human life. A pregnancy lasts nine months, and it carries uncertainties. In the darkness of the womb, a mysterious process unfolds that even the best calculations fail to grasp.

The wonder that parents experience in the face of a newborn child comes only after a nine-month period of gestation. Wonder takes time. It allows life to unfold itself. This is why abortion clinics are places of calculation, not wonder. Life becomes small, even disposable, in calculation. It grows in wonder.

Eternal life is described by Jesus as the journey of an expectant mother: "When a woman is in labor, she has pain, because her hour has come; but when she is delivered of the child, she no longer remembers the anguish, for joy that a child is born into the world" (John 16:21). The joy of tomorrow feels like pain today, but it is one and the same reality taking ever-clearer shape within the soul: the life of Jesus Christ. Vocations are born in wonder, as the Latin motto of the Integrated Humanities Program at the University of Kansas read: *Nascantur in Admiratione* ("Let them be born in wonder").

During their labor pains, young people need the companionship described since the time of Socrates as *maieutics*, the Greek term for midwifery. Socrates tells a young Theaetetus: "These are the pangs of labour, my dear Theaetetus; you have something within you which you are bringing forth." He compares himself to a midwife—one who can establish pregnancy, induce labor, calm its pain, and help deliver a healthy child. In philosophy, this means birthing a book, a love, or a great idea. For us, though, it means spiritual companionship. Each of us is a midwife to the vocation of others.

Nobody can be a midwife without entering into the time and rhythm of another person's life. In order to walk the way of each unrepeatable person, we have to give the gift of our unrepeatable time. In our consumerist culture, it's easy to think about what we spend time *on* rather than who we spend time *with*. But nothing reveals love like time.

This gift of time can't be given to programs, systems, or methods. It has to be given to persons. Let's experience the wonderful with them. Let's read the masters and practice the "gastronomy of the eyes" in front of beautiful art. Let's learn to see the commonplace with uncommon eyes, gaze at the stars, spend time in nature, and plunge ourselves into the life of Christ—the most wondrous thing of all.

A Culture of Incarnation: The Antidote to a Culture of Disincarnation

"The body, in fact, and only the body, is capable of
making visible what is invisible: the spiritual and
the divine. It has been created to transfer into the
visible reality of the world, the mystery hidden
from eternity in God, and thus to be a sign of it."

—JOHN PAUL II—
Theology of the Body

The classic 1981 film *Chariots of Fire* tells the story of Eric Liddell, a Christian runner in the 1924 Olympics. He tells his friends, "I believe God made me for a purpose, but he also made me fast! And when I run I feel his pleasure." Even if Eric did not know clearly what his purpose in life was, he knew that God made him fast—and that's a great place to start.

When do you feel God's pleasure? The Body of Christ truly needs to know. This is one of the fundamental reasons for taking the time to listen to another person's story. Eric Liddell felt God's pleasure when he ran fast. We glorify God in our bodies (1 Cor 6:20), so the most important stories that we can listen to are those of incarnate *action*. These are the stories of people glorifying God in their bodies.

We live in an increasingly disembodied world. Some in the Church have said that the Internet is the "New Areopagus"—the most important place in ancient Greece, where people met and talked—and that we should be actively engaging in it as part of the *new evangelization*. That's a nice thought. But the Greek Areopagus involved personal encounters so close that people could smell each other's sweat. Perhaps we would be wise to use our own "smell test" in order to share the gospel in a more incarnate way.

Pope Francis wrote that "realities are greater than ideas," a key principle in the development of a culture of vocation. He says that this principle "has to do with incarnation of the word and its being put into practice. . . . The principle of reality, of a word already made flesh and constantly striving to take flesh anew"[10] (*Evangelii gaudium,* no. 233). There's a dialectic between realities and ideas. When ideas become disconnected from reality, they are ineffectual at calling anyone or anything to action. They lack weight.

W.H. Auden once wrote that the "essence of prayer is paying attention." In his poem *Like a Vocation*, he starts with fantastic, idealistic images of vocation. They teach him what his vocation is not:

> Not as that dream Napoleon, rumour's dread and
> centre,
> Before who's riding all the crowds divide,
> Who dedicates a column and withdraws,
> Nor as that general favourite and breezy visitor
> To whom the weather and the ruins mean so much

He concludes that these ideas "exist in the vanishing hour." Then, there is a swift movement toward an idea of

---

[10] Pope Francis, Apostolic Exhortation on The Joy of the Gospel *Evangelii gaudium,* §49 (hereafter EG).

vocation that is rooted in a concrete reality, one that exists "somewhere always":

> But somewhere always, nowhere particularly
>> unusual,
> Almost anywhere in the landscape of water and
>> houses,
> His crying competing unsuccessfully with the cry
> Of the traffic or the birds, is always standing
> The one who needs you, that terrified
> Imaginative child who only knows you
> As what the uncles call a lie,
> But knows he has to be the future and that only
> The meek inherit the earth, and is neither
> Charming, successful, nor a crowd;
> Alone among the noise and policies of summer,
> His weeping climbs towards your life like a
>> vocation.[11]

The cries of a newborn child have called many men and women to a life of love and sacrifice. For one who has spent decades dreaming about what their vocation might look like, there is suddenly a clear duty that crawls toward their life in flesh and blood . . . like a vocation. It could be in the form of their child. It could be in the form of their neighbor. But it's always in the form of an incarnate Word, not a disembodied one.

---

[11] W.H. Auden, *Collected Poems* (New York: Modern Library, 2007), 255.

A Culture of Creativity: The Antidote to a Culture of Conformity

"Originality consists in returning to the origin."

—ANTONIO GAUDI—

Reality is more important than ideas. It's also bigger and more beautiful than ideas. If anyone should doubt this, it's enough to look at nature. There are about 298,000 species of plants on earth today and 7.8 million species of animals. Within each species there is incredible diversity—billions of distinct designs. All of the most creative minds on earth put together could not produce a world with one iota of its beauty and grandeur. J.R.R. Tolkien's Middle Earth is a vast and fascinating place in our imaginations. But if it actually existed, it would pale in comparison to the world that we actually live in.

The problem with keeping vocation in the realm of ideas is that we limit ourselves to the archetypes. We can imagine a priest (and maybe we'll even have a particularly memorable priest in mind), but not every individual priest—and certainly not the priest that a person might become if he were ordained.

Our creativity is limited, but God's is infinite. He has billions of unique vocations in mind, one for every person on earth. On a good day, we could probably name a thousand. We leave out the "long tail" of the distribution curve, but God doesn't. Somebody somewhere has a vocation that I never knew existed and could never imagine in my wildest dreams.

Conformity is a tricky thing because people don't

usually conform to realities, which are infinitely rich, but to ideas, which are often generic and shallow. Conformity, in every instance, is always conforming to something *less than* the whole person—unless it's to Christ.

In education, a lack of attentiveness to the unique person often leads teachers to put students into boxes, which encourages another form of conformity. Students are assessed and categorized from a young age according to the ideas that society has about what is valuable or not valuable. Sir Ken Robinson, in his TED Talk "Do Schools Kill Creativity?" tells the story of Gillian Lynne and her escape from a life of conformity. [12]

Gillian couldn't stop fidgeting no matter how hard she tried. The eight-year-old girl rocked vigorously in her chair and disrupted her classmates with her non-stop movement and noise. She turned in assignments late, her handwriting was poor, and she didn't seem to be following the lessons. Finally, the school sent Gillian's parents a letter recommending that she attend a special school for children with learning disorders.

Her parents first took Gillian to a specialist for an assessment to figure out what was going on. The doctor talked to her mother and observed Gillian sitting on her hands, rocking back and forth. After about twenty minutes, he asked Gillian if she would excuse them while they talked outside in the hall. Before they left the room, the doctor turned on the radio.

---

[12] Sir Ken Robinson relates the entire story in his excellent book *Element: How Finding Your Passion Changes Everything* (New York: Penguin Random House, 2009), eBook location 155.

From outside the room, they watched Gillian through a window. Within seconds after they walked out of the room, she got up and started dancing to the music. She danced in a natural, joyful way. The doctor turned to Gillian's mother and said: "You know, Mrs. Lynne, Gillian isn't sick. She's a dancer. Take her to a dance school."

Gillian enrolled in the dance school and went on to become one of the most accomplished directors and choreographers of her generation. She created some of the most successful musicals in history, including *Cats* and *Phantom of the Opera,* and was recognized for Lifetime Achievement at the 2013 Olivier Awards.

If we want to cultivate a culture of creativity, it's critical to be attentive to the unique person in front of us. We have to see the Gillians of the world sitting on their hands, rocking back and forth, tapping their fingers on the table to the beat of every song. If we're attentive, we can call them to action through the people, places, and things that move them. In some cases, it may be as easy as turning on the radio.

ACTIVE LOVE

In Dostoevsky's *The Brothers Karamazov*, a woman comes to the holy monk, Fr. Zosima, confessing that she dreams of heroic acts of love. She prefers love in dreams to love in action, and she is assailed by unbelief in God. Fr. Zosima tells her: "Strive to love your neighbor actively and indefatigably. In as far as you advance in love you will grow surer of the reality of God and of the immortality of your soul. If you attain to perfect self-forgetfulness in the love of your neighbor, then you will believe without doubt."[13]

People don't know their vocations by thinking long and hard enough about them, but through taking action—especially acts of love. A vocation is our unique way of giving and receiving love in the world, so there is no other way to fully understand it except in and through love in action.

At the end of *Pinocchio*, Pinocchio escapes Pleasure Island and returns home only to find that a giant sperm whale named Monstro swallowed his father. Geppetto is living in the belly of the whale at the bottom of the sea, and Pinocchio realizes that he has to rescue him.

There's more happening here than meets the eye. We all have to "rescue our fathers from the belly of the whale" because, from a mythological perspective, we need to recover and revivify the people and things that made us who we are. We do this not by running from the culture that formed us but by penetrating it and recovering all that is true, good, and beautiful from the forces that swallowed them.

After Pinocchio rescues his father from the belly of the whale, he is washed up and presumed dead on the beach. But it is through his sacrificial act of love that he is finally transformed into the real boy that he desired to be from the beginning. His transformation was complete.

All actions, even the worst of them, are transformative. Only *active love* fulfills a vocation, though. According to Fr. Zosima, active love is the only way that we can come to

---

[13] Fyodor Dostoyevsky, *The Brothers Karamazov* (New York: Dover Thrift, 2005), 53.

know our vocations and be convinced of the reality of God.

All five of these elements of cultural transformation—personal encounter, language, wonder, an incarnational approach, and creativity—are aimed at helping others take actions that are *ordered toward their greatest good*. Building a culture of vocation means that we love others by helping them fulfill their God-given purpose, even at a great cost—even at the cost of our own lives. There is no greater love.

Through personal encounters, we live with the "smell of the sheep," as Pope Francis often says, whether we're the pastor or part of the flock. Through our language, we proclaim truth. Through wonder, we see the sun and the stars and the dignity of our neighbor who is made in the image and likeness of God. Through the Incarnation, we touch the mystery of God in human flesh. And through creativity, we learn to taste again.

"Active love is a harsh and fearful thing compared with love in dreams," says Fr. Zosima to the dreamy woman. He continues:

> Love in dreams thirsts for immediate action, quickly performed, and with everyone watching . . . active love is labor and perseverance, and for some people, perhaps, a whole science. But I predict that even in that very moment when you see with horror that despite all your efforts, you not only have not come nearer your goal but seem to have gotten farther from it, at that very moment—I predict this to you—you will suddenly reach your goal and will clearly behold over you the wonder-working power of the

Lord, who all the while has been loving you, and all the while has been mysteriously guiding you.[14]

Through active love, we will build a culture of vocation because, despite the limits of our efforts, it will be the wonder-working power of the Lord loving and guiding us to our goal.

---

[14] The Brothers Karamazov, 55.

6

KEYS FOR GUIDING EFFECTIVE DISCERNMENT

Joshua Miller

"The fundamental objective of the formation of the lay faithful is an ever-clearer discovery of one's vocation and the ever-greater willingness to live it so as to fulfill one's mission."

—ST. JOHN PAUL II—
Christifideles Laici

FR. RAY RYLAND, may he rest in peace, was one of the most joyful men I've ever encountered. For years he was a spiritual director and mentor to me and many other people. Upon entering his office one passed a small vestibule where there was a photograph of Thomas Merton looking out with eyes so penetrating it seemed that each viewer was captivating Merton at that moment.

I noted this once to Fr. Ryland. He told me that he knew Merton, and on several occasions he had visited him at the monastery in Gethsemani. At the time of his visits, Thomas Merton was known around the world and kept up correspondence with dignitaries, writers, and politicians (Joan Baez, James Baldwin, and Erich Fromm, among others) from many countries. He was a sort of "celebrity monk" who had famous people visiting him at his monastery, Gethsemani Abbey, in Kentucky. And yet Fr. Ryland remembers being the "only one" for Thomas Merton as they sat together and talked.

The loving attentiveness that Thomas Merton gave to Fr. Ryland was a gift that Fr. Ryland gave to others. He cared for many souls and yet as we sat facing one another I was for him the "only one." At that moment Christ was calling him to give me that same loving attentiveness that Merton had given to him. I felt his love for me deeply. His light and warmth enabled me as a disciple to open up, to receive his wisdom, and to grow in Christ.

There is no technique that produces the kind of love that Fr. Ryland and others like him give. Their gaze upon Christ and active reception of His love is the only way they can provide such a loving look to others. But there are effective keys to discernment that mentors can give youth to help them discover Christ's particular love.

In the last chapter we emphasized the building of an overall culture that nurtures personal vocation. This chapter is also ordered toward that end, but here we address seven practical approaches mentors can take to help young people embrace their personal callings.

1. TEACH PERSONAL VOCATION

Pause for a moment and ask yourself: How frequently have you encountered explicit teaching on the nature of personal vocation? To what extent do we help our kids seriously identify the special project God has assigned them to build up His kingdom? How often are they challenged in our Catholic schools and from our pulpits to discover and embrace a unique vocation? How often have you heard prayers for vocations ordered exclusively toward the priesthood or religious life? If you heard a couple's excited declaration that their son "has a vocation," what would you be expected to understand by that?

Although we have clear magisterial teaching on the fundamental priority of helping each of the baptized to recognize their unique personal vocation, insufficient attention is paid to it. The focus placed on vocations to the priesthood and religious life is in many ways an understandable one. These are beautiful, vital, and immensely important vocations in terms of *states of life*. However, we can and must speak often and insistently and seriously about personal vocation. This in no way detracts from the importance of one's state of life but rather orients and lays the foundation for it.

Teaching through Language

Language is of critical importance for shaping ideas and for shaping how we think about ourselves and other people. The language we use to articulate God's love for His people in the gift of their calling is crucially significant. When we use the term "vocation" with exclusive reference to the priesthood or the religious life, the sad and direct implication is that those who are not priests or religious somehow do not have a vocation in its full sense. This is inconsistent with the teachings of the Second Vatican Council and every pope since that council, and it is harmful.

Language helps us name reality. We will have an impoverished view of reality without the proper language to name it. The Eskimos, for example, have fifty words for snow.[1] Their deep immersion in wintery climates gave birth to such nuanced vocabulary. Words are grounded in being. Language enables sight. The young Eskimo is able to see different forms of snow because he is given language for it. We see what we have words for.

Helping young people understand the very definition of personal vocation enables them to see it, grapple with it, and thus discern it better. Since chapter three is devoted to the meaning of personal vocation, I won't expound upon it here. But I will emphasize two of its key aspects that I have found especially life-giving to young people concerned about their future.

First, many young people I work with gratefully share their appreciation for learning that personal vocation is *now*—not only something to be discerned for the future—and the great impact of this realization. God's love, like his call, is in the present moment. Young people come to realize that their personal vocation right now is to be a student, to be a daughter or son, to be free from the crush of adult

---

[1] David Robson, "There really are 50 Eskimo words for 'snow,'" *The Washington Post*, January 14, 2013, available from at https://www.washingtonpost.com/national/health-science/there-really-are-50-eskimo-words-for-snow/2013/01/14/e0e3f4e0-59a0-11e2-beee-6e38f5215402_story.html?utm_term=.dc714cefb7b7.

responsibilities, to explore relationships, to make mistakes and learn from them, to explore and develop their own gifts, to grapple with all of the circumstances that teenage life presents. They realize that the time of youth is itself a calling that they should live to the full.

The effect of this awakening is twofold. First, it alleviates the anxiety that is endemic in our culture today. Young people worry about the future. They face all kinds of pressures to perform well now in preparation for some unknown life on the horizon. In addition to the drumbeat of "college preparation" sounded by high schools and grammar schools and their batteries of standardized testing, there are now exclusive kindergarten programs promising the best foundation for college success. Here, six-year-old children face enrollment interviews and the heavy expectation that failure to perform well could harm their future. For young people gripped with anxiety about life down the road, there can be happy relief knowing that they are called by God to live in the present moment of their youth.

Second, they also experience the significance and beauty of living vocationally. When young people assume (and are taught) that they are merely preparing for a future "state in life" vocation, they tend to undervalue themselves and the time of youth. They are discerning—but not actually living out—a calling. Focusing on the present vocation of youth helps them be attentive to concrete challenges and opportunities that are, in themselves, solid preparation for discerning their future calling as it unfolds.

The question "Are You Called?", so often seen on posters in the backs of churches, needs to be replaced by an imperative: "You are called. Let's help you know it and live it to the full."

2. HELP MENTEES FIND THEIR OWN WAY OF DISCERNMENT

There are common means that everyone must use in the spiritual life (prayer, sacrifice, sacraments, and others) in order to discover the Lord's will and grow in holiness. But *the primary key to discernment for each person is to find his own way of discernment.* This way is especially linked to one's unique motivational design because that design is the primordial seed of vocation—one's unique way of being.

My co-author, Luke, discovered this over several years discerning the priesthood. One of Luke's core motivations is to realize as concretely as possible the concepts and values important to him. He is a man of action, creativity, and great initiative. Luke moves quickly to put ideas not just on paper but into *direct physical practice.* In doing so, the ideas are made real to him. Although he prayed and lived close to the sacraments like the other seminarians, whenever possible Luke was out and about in Rome interacting with people in cafes and homeless shelters, exploring the arts, and keeping alive his own creative writing. When Luke neglected these things and kept to the more academic and contemplative seminarian life, his prayer dried up and he became depressed. Luke came to understand that the best way for him to figure out if God was calling him to the priesthood was to align his discernment with his unique motivational pattern. Ultimately, Luke gained clarity that

God was calling him not to be a priest but to help sanctify the world as an entrepreneur.

As a coach I have also learned the importance of orienting my clients to ways of discernment consistent with their unique motivational design. One student, Ava, is highly motivated to collaborate. She absolutely needs to have close engagement with groups of people whose values align with her own as well as strong relationships with mentors. Without such context she is like a fish out of water; she cannot see the contours of her calling. Bonnie, motivated to comprehend and express, learns God's will by turning over the rock of every possible option, studying the pros and cons of each, and then articulating what she has learned. Robert needs to be grounded in a process made up of clear steps. For him vocational decision-making requires seeing obvious connection between his current trajectory of life and possible next steps. The framework of logical forward-movement is his basic mode of being and that is the context in which he effectively discerns.

Since one's motivational design is not just a set of natural abilities but a basic orientation to be and act a certain way, its application goes beyond mere decision making. Luke and each of the clients noted above approach prayer, consideration of the world's needs, interaction with spiritual directors, and the other components of sound discernment according to their motivational design. For example, Ava, the collaborator, loves to pray through choral singing; contrast with Bonnie, the comprehender, whose prayer life is much more cerebral and meditative.

Grace perfecting nature is a principle that goes beyond

the sacraments or the gift of theological virtues. When bride and groom pledge themselves to one another, the Holy Spirit infuses their natural covenant with the supernatural sacrament of matrimony. When men learn through rational argumentation that God exists and is one, they open their minds in preparation for the gift of faith. In these situations, grace builds on or perfects nature.

The same principle applies to how God works with us in the challenge of daily discernment. If God crafts a person with a certain pattern of motivation, God will work with and perfect her according to that pattern. The way of discernment itself needs to be consistent with how the Lord has already designed the person.

The implication that one's way of discernment must be consistent with his unique motivational design is critical. For instance, a girl whose achievement stories are all about responding to needs does not require exposure to service to evoke a drive to self-gift. Her being is already oriented that way. But she might require close mentorship on how to exercise self-creative freedom and achieve the right balance between self-care and service to others. A young man whose core motivation is to bring control will be delighted to know that discerning personal vocation includes self-creative freedom, but he might balk at following other key aspects of discernment like obedience to all of God's laws or guidance from mentors. He must learn that submission to God in all things brings freedom and that conformity to truth leads to self-control.

How do you help mentees find their own way of discernment? Go to their stories. Empathic inquiry and listening open them up to share stories of personal achievement, which shed light on their motivational design. This is key to helping mentees know themselves. Mentors must help their mentees facilitate deeper self-awareness of their motivational design, which orients them not only toward their personal vocation, but helps clarify their particular way of ongoing discernment.

3. EXPLORE CONNECTION BETWEEN TALENTS AND MOTIVATIONAL DESIGN

A standard approach to vocational discernment is to figure out one's talents and then identify places in the world where there is need for those talents. The question "What should I do?" is frequently met with the counter-questions: "What are you good at?" and "What are your gifts?"

Of course it is critical for young people to discern their talents. Mentors need to spend time cultivating that awareness. One of the reasons we have emphasized exploration of achievement stories is because they usually reveal specific abilities (whether actualized or in potential) along with core motivation. Consider, for example, the stories from Benton Parker and Rachel Michaud in chapter two. Benton, who loved crooning Elvis at age eight and has had wide-ranging success in vocal competitions, clearly has talent for singing. Rachel Michaud, always sensitive to group dynamics and mission, clearly has talent for cause-oriented relationship-building that is blossoming today in her work with FOCUS.

There is often an obvious overlap between unique motivational design and talents: the mechanic driven to *make things work* has a talent for fixing broken down Harley Davidsons, and the event planner whose core motivation is to *organize* delights in arranging the thousands of logistics for weddings. Here the connection between natural ability and motivation is quite clear.

Although motivation for certain kinds of action often indicates corresponding talent, they are not the same. The movie, *Rudy*, which gives an account of the real-life Daniel "Rudy" Ruettiger, is a clear example. Rudy had a powerful drive to overcome obstacles in his quest to play football for Notre Dame but he was relatively small and unathletic. After years of getting thrashed by larger and more athletic first-stringers in his role on the Notre Dame practice squad, Rudy was allowed at the end of his senior year to suit up for a real game. His drive to overcome the odds was fulfilled and he actually got on the field for his beloved Fighting Irish—once. Rudy was motivated to play Division I college football but had little real talent to perform at that level.

Although Rudy's perseverance is notable, he exemplifies someone who has motivation for activity without corresponding talent for it. On several occasions I've worked with clients facing the opposite problem. They have talents for activities but not the motivation to cultivate or sustain those talents. One young man, who I will call "Pietro," can do a lot of things well. He's a math whiz, sings a round baritone in the choir, reads literature proficiently, creates complex computer games, and is a patient caregiver for his six younger siblings. He came to me trying to figure out what in the world he should major in at college. Engineering? Pre-Med? Communication Arts? It turns out that Pietro is fundamentally motivated to *demonstrate new learning*. The consistent theme of his achievement stories is gaining proficiency in a skill, showing he can do it well, and then moving on to a new subject. It is difficult for him to heed persistent calls to focus his studies because after gaining a degree of proficiency in one area he actually loses motivation to continue.

One solution for people like Pietro is to choose courses of study and then careers that have a built-in requirement for ongoing learning—computer programming, architecture, or multiple-subject high school teaching with coaching on the side.

Talents describe the "how" of effective activity. They are like tools in a toolbox. When there is a task that needs to be done, one can complete it well if she has talent for it. Without requisite talent, she likely cannot do it well. Core motivation gets at the "why" of activity or the underlying reason people engage in activity.

Some questioned Rudy's decision to keep seeking game time for Notre Dame given his obvious lack of qualifying athletic ability. His motivational drive to overcome obstacles was the reason; his "why" was dominant although the "how" was weak. Pietro, on the other hand, has a lot of "how"—a diverse toolbox of talents he can use to do many things well. His issue is to make sure that his motivational "why" of *demonstrating new learning* can remain engaged as he develops and deploys his talents.

Although it is important for young people and their mentors to discern talents, it is even more important to unveil their underlying core motivation. Here are a few reasons why:

- Understanding the young person's motivational design sheds light on those emerging or latent talents which particularly ought to be cultivated because of their close integration with the motivational design. For example, Pietro should develop skills enabling him to be an effective generalist, learning methods that can be applied to multiple applications.
- Settling on a course of study or career simply because of talent and without an understanding of core motivation can lead to profound stress and heartache. If Pietro got stuck in a highly specialized discipline like brain surgery just *because he could do it well*, he would be miserable.
- A young person's motivational design helps clarify the circumstances in which he will especially thrive and want to develop or exercise his talents. My son, David, is highly motivated to *excel*. He wants to win and his talents emerge in a competitive framework. David is not especially scholarly, but give him a debate tournament and he will spend hours reading academic journals and preparing briefs. Without competition he tends to lose interest and energy.

Frederick Buechner famously wrote: "The place God calls you to is the place where your deep gladness and the world's deep hunger meet."[2] This is different than stressing the connection between talent and the needs of others in discernment of personal vocation. "Deep gladness" expresses the joy of activity oriented by core motivation. The talents of young people can usually be clarified by exploring their motivational design, but the flipside is not the case. Providing young people with self-awareness of their abiding motivational design is more helpful as a key for ongoing discernment of personal vocation.

4. EXPOSE THEM TO NEED, ORIENT THEM TO SERVICE

Although we ought to recognize the needs of human beings and our world on a daily basis—"the whole creation groans" (Rom 8:22, NKJV)—it is easy for young people living comfortable lives to avoid seeing these needs. There are many reasons for this. Sometimes we steer kids away from direct exposure to the suffering of others, especially when it comes couched in danger. People living on the streets might be drunk or mentally ill. We like to keep them at a distance from our kids. We want what is best for our young people. Thus, we emphasize good education, three square meals, fun with friends, sports activities, and lots of leisure. We have service hours but these are often given and fulfilled as requirements for graduation. Kids get them done, check them off the list, and move on. At the same time, family size (about 1.5 kids per couple) and our generally urban,

---

2   Frederick Buechner, *Wishful Thinking: A Seeker's ABC* (New York: HarperOne, 1993), 118–119.

consumer-based lifestyle means children tend to grow up with what they need at their fingertips and without the experience of providing vital service for others.

Providing youth with deep experience meeting the needs of others is critical for cultivating their own callings. Mission trips can do this in a dramatic way. At Franciscan University of Steubenville, where I serve, hundreds of college students spend spring break doing works of radical service not just to the poor in other countries but to college youth partying on the sands of Daytona Beach, Florida. Many of them return awakened to what God wants of them during the next stages of their lives. The challenge of the experience draws out their gifts and clarifies how they can be used to build God's kingdom. They begin to find themselves and their callings in the radical offering of themselves.

In addition to mission trips where young people go *outside* of their own worlds, it is valuable for them to have experience *inside* their daily routines for self-gift: cleaning the home, cooking meals, doing laundry, taking care of siblings, tithing money from part-time jobs. Such chores provide the life-giving experience of making authentic contributions to others, a building block of personal vocation. At the same time, they can awaken gifts in the young person. Fine chefs often get their start in the family kitchen.

It is also important that young people directly link activities they are already motivated to do with regular acts of service. This is especially critical not primarily because they can serve (and maybe enjoy it) but because they need to understand the close integration between the *fulfillment of self* and *fulfillment of others* in God's economy. They need to know that life ought not be bifurcated between purely "I"-centered activities and "other"-centered activities. They need to grasp that in God's grand design, all members of His Body flourish when each one joyfully realizes his own purpose for the sake of the whole. As young people experience the connection between doing what is intrinsically motivating and what builds up others, they will experience the joy of giving of themselves in a full, whole-hearted way.

In all these things—traditional service activities like soup kitchen work, mundane chores, and intrinsically motivating activities—the young person's daily orientation should be: *There are needs at my school, in my home, and among my friends that I am called upon to meet. My contribution matters. My daily work is important for others. Life has meaning beyond the pursuit of pleasure.*

As you orient them toward needs, especially those that directly correspond to their motivational design, you prepare them for such an orientation.

5. HELP THEM SECURE WISE, ATTENTIVE MENTORS

"Is this me? Am I wise? Am I truly attentive to the young people under my responsibility? Do I provide what they require to effectively discern their personal vocations?" These questions, and the great need our young people have, should bring those of us who are mentors to our knees.

The wisdom that mentoring requires is not primarily practical—nor primarily born of expertise in the subject matter of a discipline. Rather, it is the wisdom born from fear of God. It is wisdom born from wonder and awe that human persons under her responsibility are unique icons of Christ that she has the privilege of helping to become who they are created to be.

My comments here relate to mentors who want to be wise and attentive in their own interactions with youth and also help those youth effectively choose other mentors who will help them make their way through life. Some mentors (I use the term broadly) will be parents, pastors, youth ministers, spiritual directors, or life coaches who directly address issues of personal discernment. Other mentors, such as those related to sports or professions, will be more focused on developing skills. In all cases the best mentors help young persons become who they are created to be, orienting them toward fully living their personal vocations.

Marks of the Wise, Attentive Mentor

What are the characteristics of mentors most effective in helping young people embrace their own unique callings?

- The wise mentor is prayerful. His eyes are aloft and his heart is open. He has a close relationship with Christ—not only a "practice" of participating in Mass or religious services and obeying the Ten Commandments but a living, personal relationship.
- The wise mentor listens and inquires with empathy. This is so critical that we devoted an entire chapter to it. Here I simply add that the effective mentor listens for potential in the young person that she

might not recognize in herself and looks for ways to draw it out.

- The wise mentor grapples with the daily call of his own personal vocation and faithfully responds to it.
- The wise mentor is self-aware and has a deep interior life. He exercises self-possession. He can name his own unique behavioral drives, and he knows how they can blossom into gift or be used for sin.
- The wise mentor reflects what he sees in the young person so she can recognize herself and what she needs for authentic growth.
- The wise mentor asks questions that prompt reflection and deepen self-awareness in the youth. He advises only when necessary and with great care so that the young person remains authentic to her personal calling and way of discernment.
- The wise mentor has been down the road of discernment before and has lots of practical, hands-on experience to pass on while avoiding the mistake of thinking that his experience is normative. The best mentors don't simply "tell it like it is" but offer insight contextualized by awareness of the mentee's personal uniqueness.
- The wise mentor focuses on helping young persons become who they are rather than swaying them to his own agenda or allowing them to walk along a self-destructive path without the challenge of tough love.

Finding Strong Mentors

One thing we can do to help our young people secure wise, attentive mentors is to gently challenge them to explore why they might be attracted to certain potential mentors over others. In our age of celebrity worship where so much value is placed on quantitative social impact—Facebook "likes" or followers on Twitter and Instagram—young people are sometimes drawn to those who are charismatic in large-group contexts, occupy high-level positions, or are well-known and popular. They might very well be effective mentors, but not necessarily. Quiet souls not in the public gaze and who prefer one-on-one encounters often make the best mentors.

In my role at Franciscan University's Center for Leadership, I serve as a personal vocation coach for a small group of students. Within a four-year period they have multiple internships and summer jobs alongside a variety of curricular and co-curricular activities. They often meet potential mentors in these various spheres of development. In order to help them secure strong mentors, I encourage them to reflect on their potential mentors and the mentoring relationship with questions like these:

- To what extent are these potential mentors grounded in a relationship with Christ?
- To what extent do they articulate and embrace their own personal vocations?
- What kind of listening is best for you to receive from mentors? Do these potential mentors truly listen to you?

- What sorts of questions help you to deeply reflect? Do they ask these questions?
- To what extent do they promote their own agenda and interests?
- To what extent do they concentrate on your development for its own sake?
- What draws you to the mentor?
- What is the connection between your own personal vocation (as far as you understand it) and this potential mentoring relationship?
- What kind of chemistry do you need to have with those who are mentoring you? Are you experiencing that kind of chemistry?
- To what extent is their advice helpful?
- Do they help you recognize your potential to identify sins to root out?
- To what extent do they strive to understand you?

Some students are sufficiently self-aware to answer such questions directly and reflectively. Others are not. That's okay. The questions themselves stimulate recognition of the issues at stake in effective mentorship. Gentle questioning can prompt young people to dig further, to raise their awareness about what is involved in mentorship and approach potential mentoring relationships with the degree of seriousness it warrants.

6. CULTIVATE PRAYERFUL SILENCE AND LISTENING

Of all the keys to effective discernment we have discussed in this chapter, prayerful silence and listening are perhaps the most important. It is absolutely critical for mentors to be grounded in these habits. We cannot pass on what we do not have. And mentees cannot hope to hear God's call without quieting and opening their own interior world. Silence is essential for receiving the Lord's voice, accepting wise counsel from others, and listening to the longing of their own hearts.

Silence is becoming more and more difficult. Modernity has for centuries emphasized the tangible over the intangible, the body over the soul. This basic cultural orientation already undermines a disposition of prayerful attentiveness, a spiritual reality.

Today's young people are faced with far greater challenges than those of the Industrial Revolution who confronted factory noise and automobiles. Contemporary youth find themselves not just surrounded by machines but plugged into them in every sphere of activity. Education, entertainment, communication, and relationship-building are mediated through technology.

Constant digitized engagement distracts us profoundly and damages our capacity for attentive silence. Many of us have felt this damage—we find it difficult now after years of interaction with computer screens to hold lengthy conversations or read books for long stretches of time. These concerns are now well documented. Books like *The Shal-*

lows: What the Internet is Doing to our Brains by Nicholas Carr, *Alone Together: Why We Expect More from Technology & Less from Each Other* by Sherry Turkle, and *You Are Not a Gadget* by Jerald Lanier are showing indisputable linkage between massive internet use and lack of capacity for deep thought, emotional blindness, inability to relate face-to-face with other human persons, along with skyrocketing rates of depression and anxiety.

Nicholas Carr details the connection between digitized distraction and functional damage to our capacity for silence. The brain, he explains, is an organ that can literally morph at the neurological level over time depending upon the kind of input it receives. We problem solve and make decisions via the pre-frontal cortex. Given the need for fast decision making while gaming or surfing the web, it makes sense that the pre-frontal cortex with its functional working memory would actually be strengthened through internet use. This has been experimentally proven. But those parts of the brain associated with long-term memory correspondingly weaken. This is because long-term memory requires slow and steady input from working memory. If working memory is blitzed with data, information transfer into long-term memory is impeded. This is precisely what happens when the pre-frontal cortex is hyper-activated in today's fast-speed digital environment; it literally weakens that part of the brain connected to long-term memory.

This is an alarming problem since long-term memory is where the brain holds its overarching conceptual schema of the world. It's where we hold together various parts of the world with an understanding of how they relate to other parts, and thus it's the place where we hold a sense of our life's meaning. It is long-term memory to which Romano Guardini refers when he says that "memory is the power with which man summons his interior world for inspection, thus for the first time really possessing himself of it." Without long-term memory we flit about from one sensual engagement with the world to another without interior depth.

There are several major effects this lack of silence has upon a young person's ability to effectively discern personal vocation. If prayer is silent conversation with God, who guides in the depths of one's interior in a "still small voice" (1 Kings 19:12), then I cannot hope to hear His voice and gain His guidance unless I step away from the noise and gain capacity for silent prayer. Sensitivity to the voice of God—awareness of His calling—is born from habits of interaction with Him. Just as I cannot learn the ways of another human person without ample time for fellowship, so I cannot learn God's ways in my life unless I spend time with Him listening to Him and engaging Him. This depends on habits of silent prayer.

I need to understand the longings of my heart, including my distinct pattern of motivation and the day-to-day desires that orient me. I need also to grasp what it means to have peace of heart which, as so many spiritual masters have indicated, is critical to understanding the Lord's will.[3]

What can mentors do to help the young people under their care gain capacity for prayerful silence and listening? In the first place, we must model it and provide our

---

[3] Jacques Philippe, *Searching for and Maintaining Peace: a Small Treatise on Peace of Heart* (New York: Alba House, 2002).

mentees with the experience of encountering them according to it. Gazing upon the young person with empathic love, asking questions that demand reflection, and listening with depth of interior life will give youth a living encounter with silence. That loving gaze declares to the young person: "You have great dignity within yourself."

Create times and places for silent prayer without fearing that the experience will be boring or not "relevant." Silent retreats where cell phones are dropped in a box at the start are a powerful mode of facilitating attentive listening in the heart of the young person. A former student from Franciscan University recently came back from mission in Russia compelled to "preach the *poustinia*" to his peers. The *poustinia*, which originates in Eastern Christian spirituality, is a form of prayer where one goes in silence to a single cabin or room that consists only of a bed, a table and chair, a cross and a Bible.

Reclaim conversation. Press for one-on-one and small-group discussion oriented to questions that invite reflective depth. Classes where young people sit face-to-face often powerfully facilitate good conversation. One exercise I have found consistently helpful in generating rich dialogue is to have youth share achievement stories in pairs of two, where each has a turn to take on the role of question-asker and story-teller. In this context they reveal themselves in authentic action to one another. Besides basic sharing, I also ask them to reflect on what they saw in one another as they express their stories, which leads to moments of mutual empathy. The whole room is typically animated with a buzz of joyful engagement and smiling faces.

7. AWAKEN THEM TO SELF-CREATIVE FREEDOM

"It's pretty easy, really," a priest once told me with regard to discerning God's will.

"Easy?" I asked.

"Yes. You pray for God's will. You consider possible choices. Then you make a decision and go for it."

I didn't argue about how "possible choices" can trip us up. I got the basic point and was struck both by its refreshing simplicity and emphasis on the power we have, by God's grace, in our own action.

Young people who want to understand the Lord's will can be anxious about the future as they stare into a myriad of possible life courses. Having various options is one reason for concern, but the deeper reason stems from failure to embrace a critical aspect of their own nature. Young people are often not aware that they image God through their own freedom, which means that doing God's will involves taking initiative, making decisions and acting on them.

Youth sometimes assume that the Lord wants them to discern in passivity, that authentic spirituality is waiting for God to tell them what to do. They can grow agitated when they hear nothing. Of course sometimes God overtly directs, and at all times He wants us to rely upon Him in prayer. But it is also true that He desires us to exercise our own freedom and to co-create our personal vocations with Him.

John Paul II's *Letter to the Youth of the World* serves as

a kind of recapitulation of key principles we have discussed in this chapter while highlighting the profound role of self-creative freedom in discernment. I quote the following passage at length because of its importance:

> Hence during youth a person puts the question, "What must I do?" not only to himself and to other people from whom he can expect an answer, especially his parents and teachers, but he puts it also to God, as his Creator and Father. He puts it in the context of this particular interior sphere in which he has learned to be in a close relationship with God, above all in prayer. He therefore asks God: "What must I do?, what is your plan for my life? Your creative, fatherly plan? What is your will? I wish to do it."

> In this context the "plan" takes on the meaning of a "life vocation," as something which is entrusted by God to an individual as a task. Young people, entering into themselves and at the same time entering into conversation with Christ in prayer, desire as it were to read the eternal thought which God the Creator and Father has in their regard. They then become convinced that the task assigned to them by God is left completely to their own freedom, and at the same time is determined by various circumstances of an interior and exterior nature. Examining these circumstances, the young person, boy or girl, constructs his or her plan of life and at

the same time recognizes this plan as the vocation to which God is calling him or her.[4]

Young people in the throes of vocational discernment often read this passage in wonder and amazement. They recognize themselves in those searching questions, "What must I do? What is your plan for my life?" The pope is not speaking here of broad cultural issues or theological principles but comes alongside their own journey. He enters into it and they enter into his good counsel. As they dwell with it they recognize in themselves the disconnect between intrinsic striving for action and an opinion that doing God's will involves waiting for Him to direct. That God wants them to construct their life plan and actually makes it His own will serves to lift the burden of that false opinion and motivate the young person's drive for action.

Cultivating effective discernment involves awakening mentees to the reality that they can literally co-create their own personal vocation. Effective mentors can draw on the teaching presented in St. John Paul II's *Letter to the Youth of the World* and others like it to catalyze this kind of enlightenment. Of course this teaching must be balanced by other key principles of discernment also addressed in the passage.

One's vocation is an individual life task, not simply a basic state in life or a general call to holiness. God has something for each one to do uniquely. To discover it, young people must be in close relationship with God and seek His

---

[4] Pope John Paul II, Apostolic Letter to the Youth of the World *Dilecti Amici* (March 31, 1985), §9.

desires through attentive prayer. They are free in proportion to their reliance on Him and conformity to His commandments. They seek good counsel from parents and teachers and other mentors. They explore "exterior circumstances" which especially include the needs of others and the historical and social contexts in which they find themselves. They examine "interior circumstances," the energetic striving of their unique patterns of motivation and the talents that flow from them. And then, while continuing in prayer, they decide on a plan of action and, in the words of my priest friend, they "go for it."

When all of these keys to effective discernment have been taken into account and there is still some uncertainty on the part of the mentee (there will always be, for most people), then one can heed the advice of Joan of Arc: "Act, and God will act."

7

MISSION

The Outward Thrust of Vocation

Luke Burgis

"My joy will not be lasting unless it is the joy of all.
I will not pass through the battlefields with a rose
in my hand."

—HENRI DE LUBAC—
Catholicisme

THERE'S NO JOY in naval gazing. But in today's
culture of *me*, even vocation can become self-referential.

For a number of years, I was a full-time, professional
vocation-discerner. From behind the walls of a seminary, I
prayed for some kind of confirmation that I was called to be
a priest. Little by little, though, the question of my vocation
became the center of my universe. "What does God want?"
I wondered. Meanwhile, voicemails on my phone piled up.
I thought that *my* vocation was (naturally) about me—the
plan for my life, the path that I would walk, the way that I
would find personal fulfillment. But I learned that a voca-

tion is not a movement *from, away*, and *in*. It's a movement *for*, *toward*, and *out*.

Joy is the fruit of love, and love is the fruit of communion. Pope Benedict XVI reflected on this social aspect of salvation in his encyclical *Saved in Hope*. "How did we arrive at this interpretation of the 'salvation of the soul' as a flight from responsibility for the whole?" he asks.

This flight is antithetical to salvation and so also to vocation. A person is saved by responding to the call of Christ with faith and living out his life in response to that call—in other words, living out his vocation, which unites him to Christ in a singularly personal way. How can we be indifferent to the vocation of our brother, then? His very salvation depends on it. Our joy depends on it.

Army medic Desmond Doss, portrayed in the 2016 film *Hacksaw Ridge*, lived out the missionary aspect of his vocation heroically. During one of the bloodiest battles of World War II, he refused to even carry a gun. He was armed only with faith in God, a pocket Bible, and the conviction that he must fulfill his duties as a medic without taking a life. (Doss was a Seventh Day Adventist with a strict interpretation of the fifth commandment, "Thou shalt not kill.") He believed his duty was to serve God and to serve his country—in that order.

During the Battle of Okinawa, Doss' company of soldiers was on a mission to overtake enemy territory above an imposing rock face nicknamed Hacksaw Ridge. Thousands of Japanese soldiers were waiting for them. When Doss and his team got to the top of the ridge, they came under a barrage of mortar and machine gun fire so heavy that the Japanese called it the "rain of steel."

Hundreds of American troops lay wounded and dying. Corporal Doss crawled over the rocky terrain from soldier to soldier, providing immediate first aid. In the Medal of Honor award ceremony for Doss, President Harry S. Truman said, "Private First Class Doss refused to seek cover and remained in the fire-swept area with the many stricken, carrying them one by one to the edge of the escarpment and there lowering them on a rope-supported litter down the face of a cliff to friendly hands."[1] When the battle was over, he'd rescued at least seventy-five soldiers. Doss was a one-man field hospital.

Pope Francis used the image of a field hospital to describe the Church's missionary dimension. "I prefer a Church which is bruised, hurting and dirty because it has been out on the streets rather than a Church which is unhealthy from being confined and from clinging to its own security" (EG §49).

The Pope thinks a Church that does not go out into the world becomes sick from atrophy, like a person who spends a month on bedrest. If the Church goes out to the streets, it grows through unexpected encounters and challenges. That Church becomes "antifragile."

Author Nassim Nicholas Taleb, an expert on risk, describes things that improve under stress as antifragile, which is the opposite of fragile. Something is fragile if it

---

[1] See the Desmond Doss Council, http://www.desmonddoss.com/medal-of-honor/.

gets weaker when it is exposed to shocks; something is antifragile if it thrives in uncertainty. "Antifragility has a singular property of allowing us to deal with the unknown, to do things without understanding them—and do them well," Taleb writes.[2]

Antifragile things stand the test of time: evolution, culture, ideas, political systems, and good recipes (like flat bread with toppings—better known as pizza[3]). Nature is quintessentially antifragile. So is the Church and, necessarily, so are we. "The blood of the martyrs is the seed of the Church," wrote the early Christian apologist Tertullian (d. 220). History is a witness to the antifragility of the Church.

Fearful self-preservation is unhealthy for the Church, and for each of her members. Jesus told His disciples, "Truly, truly, I say to you, unless a grain of wheat falls into the earth and dies, it remains alone; but if it dies, it bears much fruit" (John 12:24). In our work of cultivating vocations, we have to give young people the freedom to fall. We have to encourage them to take risks for love, and to go forth boldly with the conviction that those who walk with Christ are not only antifragile—they're "made perfect in weakness" (2 Cor 12:9).

My friend Michael recently told me about taking his ten-year-old son, Joey, skiing on an advanced, black diamond trail for the first time. He stood on the top of the mountain in Jackson Hole, Wyoming, and watched his son navigate his way down the mountain before disappearing around a bend. They had run the blue square and green

---

[2] Nassim Nicholas Taleb, *Antifragile: Things That Gain from Disorder (Incerto)* (New York: Random House, 2014), 4.

[3] Included in the cookbook of the ancient Roman recipe-writer Apicius.

circle trails together hundreds of times, talking about the best way to turn, take moguls, and stop on a dime. But at that moment, as he watched Joey disappear, Michael knew that Joey was on his own. Sink or swim. Fall or ski. Break a leg or (hopefully) not. Joey needed to risk failure in order to learn things that he would never learn with his father's hand on his shoulder.

If we don't risk anything, we risk everything. Living a vocation requires facing uncertainty and danger. But vocations aren't lived, or even discerned, in comfort. They're forged on mission.

VOCATION AND MISSION

"God called Abraham and commanded him to go
out from the country where he was living. With
this call God has roused us all, and now we have
left the state."

—ST. JUSTIN MARTYR—

In the *exitus-reditus* of salvation history, or sending forth and returning of all things to the Creator, vocation and mission come together in a singular journey back to the heart of the Father.

My friend Daniel remembers his father rocking in a big chair on the back porch of their southwest Louisiana farmhouse. He sipped tepid Sunkist orange soda (to maximize the orange-ness) and smoked a pipe packed with Scotty's Butternut Barley tobacco. Daniel and his siblings Mark and Marissa could smell the sweet honey and vanilla aroma from the end of their hundred-yard-long driveway. Around seven every night, their dad stood up and called his children in from the fields. "Dinner's ready!" He rang a bell in case the kids had wandered beyond the range of his booming voice.

When they heard the call, Daniel, Mark, and Marissa each took their own paths back home. Each path had unique terrain to navigate. Daniel crossed the creek from the far bank where he would dig for crawfish. Marissa jumped off the swing and ran her friend home down the street before circling back to the house. And the youngest, Mark, would climb down from whatever tree he was in and sprint across the field, avoiding any molehills. The first one in the door got a piece of hot bread straight out of the oven. There were many paths, but one call.

A vocation is the unique pathway that each person is called to travel back to the Father, which is the ultimate mission of every Christian. "The fundamental objective of the formation of the lay faithful is an ever-clearer discovery of one's vocation and the ever-greater willingness to live it so as to fulfill one's mission," wrote John Paul II (CL §58). Without a doubt, our final mission is entrance into eternal life with God through death.

But along each pathway, there are unique missions that the traveler must undertake in order to reach the end of the path—in order to live out his vocation and fulfill his mission. In *The Lord of the Rings*, Frodo Baggins' mission is to destroy the One Ring in the fires of Mount Doom in Mordor. This is what he must do to live out his vocation. Along the journey Frodo and his eight companions (the

Fellowship of the Ring—those who walk with him on his journey) encounter many obstacles that they must overcome in order to fulfill the mission. These, too, are missions.

There's an intimate connection between a person's missions and his vocation, the way that he returns to the Father. Pope Benedict wrote, "The *exitus* (going out) . . . is indeed ordered toward the *reditus* (return)." Missions are ordered to the return to the Father, which begins with the call to follow Christ—the primary and fundamental mission of every Christian.

UNIVERSAL MISSION

Following Christ is, in itself, a multidimensional mission. All of the baptized follow Christ by sharing in the three missions that Christ fulfilled in His work of salvation: the priestly, prophetic, and kingly.

Priestly Mission. As sharers in his *priestly mission*, the lay faithful are able to offer their daily activities to the Father for the sanctification of the world. A well-written legal brief, the preparation of a family dinner, and a student's diligent study time all affect the transformation of the world in Christ when they are accomplished in the Spirit. Ordinary activities are not trivial—they are the hinges on which holiness turns, the mission of every person to offer spiritual sacrifices to the Father through Jesus Christ.

Prophetic Mission. Through their participation in the *prophetic mission* of Christ, the faithful are charged with the mission of proclaiming the Gospel in word and deed in the midst of the world. In order to bear the truth of God to the world, the prophetic mission challenges all of the baptized faithful to earnestly seek and share the truth with others, even when it is difficult.

Kingly Mission. As sharers in the *kingly mission* of Christ, the faithful are called to establish his kingdom of love firmly in their lives, displacing the kingdom of sin and working to establish Christ's reign of peace throughout history. The kingly mission includes the ordering of our lives and communities toward truth. A Catholic mother directs her children toward the fulfillment of their God-given vocations, and a Catholic politician governs a city with a full appreciation of the moral dimension of his work.

Above all, writes Pope John Paul II, "the lay faithful are called to restore to creation all its original value" (CL §14). They are called to enter the stream of the *reditus* and bring all of creation with them.

These missions of Christ manifest themselves in many and varied ways in the circumstances of daily life. In sincerely following Christ, all of our "particular" missions reveal themselves.

PARTICULAR MISSIONS

Timothy Burke learned the meaning of mission by accepting hundreds of them over the course of his twenty-three-year career in the United States military, twenty-one of those in special operations. Tim served for many years with 1st SFOD-D (Delta Force), and was deployed on hundreds of missions throughout the world as a Delta Force warrior, the U.S. military's most elite special operations unit. He saw combat in Iraq, Columbia, and Haiti.

I met Tim through my friend and business partner David Jack, who worked with Tim training executives of U.S. companies to be more effective leaders. A few years ago, the three of us walked the streets of downtown Las Vegas at night to discuss a new business initiative. Downtown Las Vegas is not the safest part of town. But with Tim's head on a swivel (he is also the designer of the U.S. military's Special Forces Advanced Urban Combat Course), I felt safe.

I recently reconnected with Tim to ask him about the importance of missions and the role that they play in living out a vocation. Tim's personal calling, which included his service in the U.S. Army, required him to complete many missions to remain faithful to his vocation. And now, in his retirement, he takes on different kinds of missions. He appreciates what he learned from his time in combat and how those missions helped to shape the person that he is today. There are at least three ways that being on mission helps to live out a vocation.

Preparation

A clear mission is often the difference between life and death for a solider. If Tim went into enemy territory without a clearly defined mission, he would be unprepared and unaware of what needed to be done in order to win the battle. This is especially true in the spiritual life. Jesus told His disciples, "Or what king, going to encounter another king in war, will not sit down first and take counsel whether he is able with ten thousand to meet him who comes against him with twenty thousand?" (Luke 14:31).

Tim describes mission as something all-encompassing. When he knows what mission he is on, he begins to see everything through the lens of that mission so that he can prepare accordingly. When I talked to him, Tim was preparing for a new Survivor-style reality T.V. show where he would have to survive on a remote desert island in Indonesia for sixty days. "Every waking moment for two months now, I have thought about surviving in a primitive environment," he told me. "The other day, performing hurricane clean up, I was noticing the bushes, the berries in the bushes, the leaf forms and shapes, constantly asking myself, 'Are these edible? What do I know about this plant? Can it be used to make a roof, a wall, a bowl, or some utensil?'"

Tim's latest mission gave him a way to interpret his daily experiences in the light of his mission, even while helping with Hurricane Irma relief in Florida. While thousands had been involved in the hurricane relief efforts, Tim was probably the only one considering the edibility of plants and leaves in order to be able to survive on a remote island. He assimilated the experience in a unique way that allowed him to prepare for one mission even the midst of another.

In the *Unrepeatable Life* workbook, there are exercises aimed at helping young people prepare for a future mission—even one as simple as "going to school tomorrow"—starting with what they are doing at this moment. Mission is all-encompassing, like the personal vocation that it serves. It touches everything and every moment.

Focus

In the military, Tim used a Mission Essential Task List (METL) to determine how he was going to train for an upcoming deployment or mission. "Having a mission causes me to viciously prioritize," he told me. "It becomes very clear what is both important and urgent, and gives me perspective on what isn't urgent or worthy of my attention."

It's critical to separate the essential from the non-essential. Tim's Mission Essential Task List when he was preparing to go to Iraq started with the recognition that he needed to prepare for combat. Tim explains what that means.

1. I will have to shoot my gun.
2. I will have to throw grenades.
3. I will have to shoot armor destroying rockets like a Karl Gustov.
4. I will have to make communications with sophisticated equipment.
5. I will have to treat wounded.
6. I will have to simultaneously command my troops on the ground while talking to aircraft loitering in support of our tactical movements.
7. I will have to maintain my leadership, professionalism, and poise, and know at all times that I am being watched by my men, who are developing their inner

dialogue of how to act in given situations based on my behavior.

This focus gave a sense of direction to Tim's life. A mission isn't a set of instructions. It takes on a life of its own and gives a leader a clear sense of what he should be doing *right now*.

God doesn't will that everyone focuses on everything at all times, but that each person focuses on that which is given to him in order to live out his vocation. There is great freedom in this.

Action-Oriented

Mission inspires when it is aligned with a person's core motivational drive. "Mission invigorates me," Tim said. "I'm sharper, I have a quicker wit, and I'm more perceptive and much quicker to engage. . . . I'm hyper-focused, energized, decisive." This is the kind of language that we regularly hear in Achievement Stories. They are almost always stories of people *going out* of themselves in order to accomplish a mission and do something inherently good. The stories reveal not only a pattern of motivational drive but also a pattern of missionary activity in a person's life.

To create a culture of vocation, we should strive to be biographers of each other. "To discover the presence of God in our individual stories . . . this is the great turning-point that transforms our merely human outlook," wrote John Paul II.[4]

4 Pope John Paul II, Message in anticipation for the XXXVIII World Day of Prayer for Vocations, September 25, 2000.

We must listen attentively to others and help them to name the graces that we see in their stories—God working in their lives—which they may have never noticed themselves. In doing this, we help them to enter into the narrative arc of their story. We help them grasp their mission.

In a great work of literature or film, every character has a mission—something that they really want is driving the plot line. It's not always obvious. But through the smoke, if you look hard enough, you see that every character acts to achieve some purpose. Of course, these missions are not always good. An evil character will have an evil mission. In God's drama of salvation history, though, each person's mission is fundamentally good and inseparable from his vocation. If we look and listen closely to the action that is driving their plot, we can help them uncover this God-given mission.

The Aristotelian-Thomistic axiom, *Agere sequitur esse* ("Action follows being"), which underlies our biographical approach, means that a person's actions both reveal and determine who he is. We become what we do, and we do what we've become. If you want to understand who a person is, don't focus on what they say. Focus on what they do.

Tim summed up this connection between the action-oriented nature of mission and its effect on a person: "Mission isn't something you do, it is someone you become." A vocation is a call to *become who you are* through the actions that you undertake to fulfill your mission.

MISSIONARY DISCIPLES

"Every Christian is a missionary to the extent that
he or she has encountered the love of God in
Christ Jesus: we no longer say that we are 'disciples'
and 'missionaries,' but rather that we are always
'missionary disciples.'"

—POPE FRANCIS—
Evangelii Gaudium

The importance of crafting a mission statement is central to business school dogma. Entire books have been written on how to craft the perfect statement. I spent some of my young adult life reading those books. "Make it less than ten words," "make it measurable," and "make it audacious" are a few of the common tenants. I started four companies before I realized that they're wrong.

Pope Francis, at a youth meeting on vocation, told attendees to repeat frequently that "I am on a mission" and not simply that "I have a mission." Missions are not statements. They're lived realities. We can't know what our mission is until we've taken the first step. In other words, we can't know our mission until we're already on it. Our job is to identify it—and that is not something that we can do alone.

In my experience as an entrepreneur, companies don't start with a mission statement. They start by responding to a need. Later, after the founders and team members reflect on what it is they are doing, they are able to articulate a mission based on the meaning that they find in what they are doing and its ultimate human value. The organization thrives if each of its members makes the mission of the organization personal, discovering his or her unique role within the organizational mission.

In the Church, every member of Christ's Body shares in His one mission of salvation. In accepting the missions of ordinary, daily life (Madeleine Delbrêl called them "faithful superiors" which we must obey), a picture begins to form of how each person is being called to contribute to Christ's work of salvation, which means sanctifying the small piece of the world that has been entrusted to them. Some people will transform a kitchen into a place of communion. Others will look at a pile of bricks and glorify God. "A rock pile ceases to be a rock pile the moment a single man contemplates it, bearing within him the image of a cathedral," wrote Antoine de Saint-Exupéry.[5]

St. Ignatius, the master of discernment, does not pose the question of vocation abstractly. He doesn't ask, "Do I have a vocation?" He asks, "What should I do, I myself, today?" By focusing on the concrete things that God is calling us to do right here and now—our little missions— we gain a deeper understanding of our personal vocation.

If a child has any anxiety about what his mission in the world is, he should start by making his bed. Then he should clean his room. Little things are the stuff that the spiritual life is made of, and every journey begins with a first step. "[Y]ou have been faithful over a little, I will set you over much; enter into the joy of your master" (Matt 25:23).

---

[5] Antoine de Saint-Exupéry, *Flight to Arras* (Boston: Mariner Books, 1969), 129.

Attentiveness to little things brings discernment out of the abstract and into the concrete reality of daily life.

Young people have hundreds of opportunities to exercise a spirit of discernment. But in order for that to happen successfully, there has to also be time for recollection (literally, a re-collecting of the pieces of experience into a unified whole). For every going out, there must be a going in.

Missionary disciples are formed when there is both *mission* (sending out) and *discipleship* (being with the Lord). The evangelist Luke writes, "The seventy returned with joy, saying, 'Lord, even the demons are subject to us in your name!'" (Luke 10:17). The disciples were sent out on a mission, but they returned to the feet of the Master. Like blood with a well-functioning heart, a missionary disciple *goes out* and *returns*. Both are essential. We measure systolic and diastolic blood pressure. What about our systolic and diastolic missionary impulses?

Cultivating vocations must involve both directions. Until now, it seems that discernment tends toward one or the other extreme. On the one hand, young Christians often enter a "period of discernment" and focus on discerning their vocation in a way that quickly becomes self-referential if it is not accompanied by an outward movement. On the other hand, thousands of high school graduates go overseas to teach English or drill wells in Africa without having learned to develop the inward reflection needed to make sense of all of their experiences before God. We need to give young people an opportunity to engage both aspects of missionary discipleship.

A Mission Year

"I dream of a missionary option," wrote Pope Francis, "that is, a missionary impulse capable of transforming everything." We dream of a very specific way to give every young person a "missionary option": a *Mission Year* opportunity for every high school graduate.

In the secular world, Gap Years have become extremely popular. Many students take a year between high school and college to travel, work, or engage in charitable activities. The overwhelming majority of them report their Gap Year to be a positive, life-changing experience. Still, there is often no way for them to know how to make sense of it all and where to go from there. Amy Peterson, author of *Dangerous Territory: My Misguided Quest to Save the World*, tells the story of her missionary journey to a foreign land as one without guidance. We are the guides that our children rely on.

We imagine a Mission Year imbued with a spirit of discernment and a series of missionary experiences in our local towns and communities—internships, jobs, and volunteer work in a variety of circumstances tailored to each person. It will help young people acquire basic skills of discernment, to understand their gifts and charisms, to learn how to live in community, and to take a step back from the frantic pace of the educational system that most of them are thrust into from age five. Most importantly, it would help each of them to discover, embrace, and live out their unique personal vocation.

Young people graduate from high school and make major life decisions—college, course of study, career trajectory, and marriage—without having learned basic habits of discernment. In the Catholic Church, most seminarians go through six to nine years of formation surrounded by priests and peers who support them, while laity are often expected to fend for themselves in their discernment process. A year of service-oriented action and guided spiritual discernment would give young people a trove of competencies that they can draw from for the rest of their lives.

The Mission Year could be organized at the church, diocesan, or community level and include a variety of active experiences—work, volunteering, recreation—tailored to each individual based on their unique motivational design and interests. Those activities would be supplemented by independent and group study of relevant topics, vocational coaching, peer support groups, and spiritual direction. For instance, there could be part-time work or service in an area of interest (and motivation) Monday–Wednesday, peer meetings and study on Thursday, prayer and spiritual direction on Friday, recreation and service with other members of the program on Saturday, and rest and worship on Sunday.

John Paul II wrote to Christian parents, teachers, and educators about the importance of their role as cultivators of personal vocation: "Their task is to guide the young generations towards discovering the plan of God for each of them, cultivating in them the readiness, when God calls them, to turn their lives into a gift for that mission."[6] The Mission Year would be a privileged place to work together toward that end.

---

[6] Address in anticipation of World Day of Prayer for Vocations.

As a service-oriented program, the Mission Year will help young people answer the question, "What is my life for?" but also *Who is my life for?*

MISSION TERRITORY

"Thérèse of Lisieux's mission covered a mere few square meters, in order to teach us that the effectiveness of a mission is not always measurable by the hands of a clock, that actions are not always visible, that missions covering vast distances will be joined by missions that penetrate straight into the depth of the crowds of humanity."

—MADELEINE DELBRÊL—
The Marxist City as Mission Territory

Each person—unique and unrepeatable—is the way for the Church. As missionaries of vocation, we're not primarily missionaries "to the nations," to industries, or to schools. We're missionaries to people.

The world desperately needs missionaries who are willing to go into the mission territory of each person's life. The human person, as the center of civilization and culture and for whom civilization and culture exist, is always the primary mission territory.

This is one of the hardest forms of missionary work there is because we are, from the first moment of our lives, the center of our own existence. We think, feel, and experience things from a first-person perspective. Even a missionary who goes halfway around the world can do so without ever leaving the comfort of his own little world.

"The missionary spirit is not only about geographical territories," Pope Francis said at World Mission Day 2013, "but about peoples, cultures and individuals, because the 'boundaries' of faith do not only cross places and human traditions, but the heart of each man and each woman."

Aleksandr Solzhenitsyn, author of *The Gulag Archipelago*, learned about the missionary territory of the heart in the forced labor camps of Siberia: "If only it were all so simple! If only there were evil people somewhere insidiously committing evil deeds, and it were necessary only to separate them from the rest of us and destroy them. But the line dividing good and evil cuts through the heart of every human being."[7]

The primary missionary territory is the heart of every human being. On our missionary journey, we can't be afraid to cross over the boundaries—the dividing lines deep within our hearts. Conversions aren't complete until the entire person is transformed. C. S. Lewis often said that G. K. Chesterton baptized his intellect, and the writing of George MacDonald baptized his imagination. He was transformed gradually until the light of Christ permeated his entire existence, including his heart.

It's difficult to be missionaries to others because we are dealing with invisible realities that only become visible from time to time. The territory of a person's life is not an open book. You hit it off with a new friend. You meet up weekly

---

[7] Aleksandr Solzhenitsyn, *The Gulag Archipelago* (New York: Collins & Harvill Press, 1973), 168.

for coffee, you play sports together, and you get together on special occasions. One day, though, you talk politics for the first time. During the conversation, his face turns bright red and he yells in your face and leaves. That's unexplored territory.

Imagine if you had a map of the interior life of every person that you know. You'd quickly find that there were certain territories of the map that you spent most of your time in. There would be other parts of the map, like foreign countries, that you hardly ever traveled to. And there would be other parts of the map that were simply blacked out, with a big red sign that read, "Off Limits."

In order to be a missionary to persons, we have to be willing to explore as much of the maps of other people as they are willing to allow us to explore—even up to the boundaries, or peripheries, of their visible territory. Throughout history, peripheries have been God's preferred place to work.

In his missionary exhortations, Pope Francis often speaks about "going out to the peripheries." The word "periphery" comes from the Greek word *periphéreia*, which means "circumference." In geometry, the peripheries are the outer boundaries of a circle. In the Dynamic Model of Vocation, the "circular movement of vocation" is represented by a circle because it shows the outward thrust of vocation from our unique motivational core outward, toward the peripheries, where we encounter not only the people to whom the Lord sends us as missionaries but also our deepest identity in Christ.

Christ Himself leads us on the outward movement (literally, *ecstasy*) to the peripheries of human existence where we encounter pain, misunderstanding, fear, loneliness, and failure. When we arrive on the peripheries, we find that we've been traveling the circular journey of vocation. Like the man who set out from his village and wound his way up the mountain, we arrive at the end of our journey and look back at the place where we set out and see that it is where we wanted to be all along—the Father's house.

Pope St. John Paul II summed up the great promise that being a missionary holds: "Jesus Christ is the chief way for the Church. He himself is our way 'to the Father's house' and is the way to each man. On this way leading from Christ to man, on this way on which Christ unites himself with each man, nobody can halt the Church" (RH §13).

One who walks the way of Christ is on a path leading to each person. At the end of his journey, when he arrives at the Father's house, he will be welcomed by a vast throng of people whom he has walked with at various stretches of the path.

His joy is complete.

EPILOGUE

A Prayer for Personal Vocation

"Simon Peter said to them, 'I am going fishing.'
They said to him, 'We will go with you.'"

—JOHN 21:3—

EVERY NIGHT, fishermen in the small town of Cetara, Italy, go out on mission. Their mission is to catch anchovies.

Cetara is fisherman's country. They've been fishing there for thousands of years (some say the name comes from the Latin *cetari*, "fishmongers"). Everyone in the town of 2,300 is either a fisherman or related to one.

The hands of the old men playing cards in the streets bear the marks of decades of fishing the Gulf of Salerno—fists that have clutched nets and cigars and held thousands of squirming and ice cold fish between their fingers.

The fishermen leave the port of Cetara around eight in the evening and stay out as long as they need in order to catch their haul for the night. It's usually two or three in the morning before they head to shore, eyes weary from the bright light they shine in the water all night to draw the anchovies to the surface.

Each fisherman has a unique role to play. There is of course the captain. Another man sets out on a smaller boat to scout for schools of anchovies and keep an eye on the large net's perimeter. The strongest men wear rainsuits and empty the thousands of anchovies from the net into large ice chests. As they return to shore, they all work together, arranging the anchovies into smaller Styrofoam cases to sell, and separating out bycatch (fish unintentionally caught) like sardines and red squid. Usually one of the fisherman's relatives pulls up to the dock as they get to shore around four or five in the morning with a refrigerated truck to haul the catch to market.

The anchovies are the pride of Cetara and some of the best in the world. Eat them *sotto sale* (under salt), *sott'olio* (under oil), fried, or any other way you can or could not ever imagine. Drizzle a little *colatura di alici,* an ancient fish sauce made from the tiniest anchovies, on your pasta.

In the Church of St. Peter, tucked in a small piazza near the port of Cetara, there's a prayer sitting in a plain picture frame atop a side altar. Its author is anonymous. Most of the fishermen, though, would probably know it by heart even if they'd never seen the prayer in their lives. They lived it.

It's the prayer of their vocation. It's the prayer that rises naturally to the lips of anyone who has spent six hours a night on a small boat in the Tyrrhenian Sea catching anchovies for the past thirty years.

I imagine that it was the prayer of Peter as he sat in his boat in the Sea of Galilee. A fisherman.

Somewhere in the world, there must be a Butcher's Prayer, a Motorcycle Mechanic's Prayer, a Politician's Prayer. Thousands.

But that's not enough. There are more. There must be about 7,484,325,476. How many will pray them?

How many will hear them?

The Fisherman's Prayer

As evening falls, we men of the sea lift up to You,
    Lord,
through the intercession of St. Peter,
patron of Cetara, our prayer
and our hearts: the living, in boats, and the dead in
    the depths of the sea.
Grant that the nights pass serenely for those who
keep watch at work,
and those who are weary may find rest.
Grant that every seaman, before sleep, be signed
    with Your sign, in Your love, in Your
Forgiveness and in fraternal peace.
Grant that every boat keep its course, and every
    seaman his faith.
Command that the wind and the waves do not test
    Our boats, and that Evil does not tempt our
    hearts.
Comfort our solitude with the memory of those
    dear to us, our melancholy with the hope of
    tomorrow, our anxieties with the assurance of
    a safe return.
Bless the families that we leave on the shore;
Bless our homeland and the homelands of all
    seamen,

that the sea may unite and not divide;
Bless those who work on the sea to earn their daily
     bread;
Bless those who rest in the depths of the sea who
     await Your Light and
     Your forgiveness.
To you, O Maria, refulgent Star of the Sea, you who
     are our light,
     our beacon, the guide, certain to direct our
     trouble hearts
     to the safe harbor of salvation in Christ, your
     Son, who lives and reigns with God the Father
     in the unity of the
     Holy Spirit, for ever and ever. Amen.

Prayer for Embracing Personal Vocation

Father of Mercy,

You called every creature into being,
> and continue to call them to Yourself through
> Your Son, Jesus Christ.

You call each person in a special way from the
> first moment of existence to an unrepeatable
> vocation,

To be priest, prophet, and king of all creation,
> to a personal mission that only he or she can
> fulfill, in order to share life with You for all
> eternity.

Lord, we beg You to grant us the graces that we
> need to continually discover, embrace, and live
> our unique, personal vocations.

As we live out our vocations, grant us the grace to
> help others live out their callings as we live out
> our own, so that the Church may be a place
> where all people can flourish according to their
> unique personal vocation in the world.

When we doubt, increase our faith in Your loving
> design,

When we are weary, strengthen us with the hope of
    heaven,
When we fail to respond fully, have mercy on us
    and call us anew, so that, filled with holy desire
    that surpasses every human longing,
    we may respond with all our mind, all our
    strength, and all our heart, to Your eternal love,
    that each of us may become who we are.
We ask this through Your Son, Jesus Christ, who
    lives and reigns with You in the unity of the
    Holy Spirit forever and ever. Amen.

APPENDIX I

About Inscape and Co-Founders Luke Burgis and Joshua Miller

IN OUR TWENTIES we were drawn fully to the Catholic faith. Joshua converted in 1998 after being a pro-life missionary and Luke embraced the faith while in the midst of a highly successful entrepreneurial career. Catholic teaching on personal vocation has been especially close to our hearts because of its emphasis on the dignity and full flourishing of every human being. It has been an important part of Joshua's work as a consultant and a coach. Luke included a strong emphasis on it when he founded *ActivPrayer*, a company devoted to fitness according to the unique design of each person.

Soon after our respective conversions we contemplated St. John Paul II's instruction that "every initiative serves true renewal in the Church . . . insofar as the initiative is based on adequate awareness of the individual Christian's vocation" (RH §21), and that "personal vocation and mission defines the dignity and responsibility of each member of the lay faithful and makes up the focal point of the whole work of formation" (CL §58). These are strong words and should be taken very seriously!

But as our experience in the daily rhythm of Catholic life continued, we began to recognize a troubling reality about the practical application of Church teaching on personal vocation. From Luke's standpoint as a seminarian (during which time he discerned his vocation to be an entrepreneur) and from Joshua's perspective as a married man and father immersed in parish life, we came to see that:

- Most discussion in the Church today about vocation refers to the priesthood and religious life or, to a lesser extent, about the importance of strong vocations to marriage.
- The very idea of personal vocation remains either an unknown or a peripheral concept for many Catholics.
- Millions of Catholic young people graduate high school and college without having had serious discussions about vocation in general, and with little or no formation in their own distinctive vocation.

This is a sad state of affairs because the renewal of the Church and the transformation of the world cannot be achieved without robust emphasis on personal vocation.

In light of this situation, we formed Inscape, an organization devoted to the vision of *each person knowing, embracing, and living to the full their unique personal vocation.*

As our story unfolds, we look forward to making it a part of your story . . . and the story of the Church.

To learn more, please visit inscapevocations.com.

APPENDIX II

Training Resources

DRAWING OUT and listening with empathy to another's stories, especially of authentically fulfilling activities, is critical for cultivating personal vocation. This process is at the heart of our assessment and training resources.

Vocation Mentor Training

An eight-hour training program that equips participants to learn the basics of personal vocation mentorship: asking powerful questions, listening with empathy, and helping young people to embrace their unique callings.

Unrepeatable Life: An Eight-Week Program Helping Young People Identify, Embrace, and Live to the Full Their Unique Personal Vocations.

In this eight-week program young people discover: (1) Their basic pattern of core motivations or unique way of loving; (2) The kinds of service to God and neighbor they have been designed to give; (3) Key principles of vocational discernment for lifelong application.

The program includes workbooks for students as well as a facilitator's guide and other teaching resources.

Additional information about all of these resources can be found at inscapevocations.com or by emailing us at coreteam@inscapevocations.com.

APPENDIX III

Additional Resources on Personal Vocation

THE FOLLOWING LIST is limited to a few titles we have found especially helpful in shedding light on the reality of personal vocation itself and practical means of discerning it.

On Personal Vocation

On the Vocation and the Mission of the Lay Faithful in the Church and in the World (Christifideles Laici), Pope Saint John Paul II, December 30, 1988.

Essential for understanding Church teaching on the lay vocation in general and that the focal point and primary objective of formation should be an "ever-clearer discovery of one's vocation and the ever-greater willingness to live it so as to fulfill one's mission" (CL §58).

Personal Vocation: God Calls Everyone By Name, Germain Grisez and Russell Shaw, Our Sunday Visitor, 2003.

This book is an apologetic for personal vocation. The

authors trace its historical development beginning with God's calling of specific people in Sacred Scripture through the documents of Vatican II, specifically those related to the lay vocation, and concluding with the full development of personal vocation in the teaching of Pope St. John Paul II. They argue that personal vocation is widely neglected and must be revitalized as a foundational part of the new evangelization.

The Personal Vocation: Transformation in Depth Through the Spiritual Exercises, Herbert Alphonso S.J., Gregorian and Biblical Press, 2006.

Fr. Alphonso beautifully describes how personal vocation is the central means of intimacy with God and that the particular daily *examen* at the heart of Jesuit spirituality is essentially a reference to one's personal vocation.

The Redeemer of Man (Redemptor Hominis) Pope St. John Paul II, 1979.

In this first encyclical of his pontificate, Pope St. John Paul II, teaches that personal vocation is key to authentic renewal in the Church and that each unique person "is the primary and fundamental way" for the Church.

On Discernment of Personal Vocation

Discerning the Will of God: An Ignatian Guide to Christian Decision Making, Fr. Timothy Gallagher O.M.V., Crossroad Publishing Company, 2009.

The Ignatian approach to discerning God's will emphasizes the value of attentiveness to the heart's authentic desires. Since one's unique motivational design is essentially a drive of the heart there is close alignment between understanding one's motivations and Ignatian discernment which is clearly and simply explained in this excellent book.

Let Your Life Speak: Listening for the Voice of Vocation, Parker Palmer, Jossey-Bass, 2000.

Parker is one of few authors who recognize that God endows each person with unique patterns of behavior and that discernment of vocation must involve listening to how these patterns speak through our life stories.

The Stories We Live: Finding God's Calling All Around Us, Kathleen Cahalan, Eerdmans, 2017.

Cahalan sheds light on the dynamic and daily nature of personal vocation. Rather than thinking of it in static terms as a noun, Cahalan shows how we can fruitfully understand our own vocation through the grammar of prepositions. Vocation is about being called *by* God, *to* follow, *as* I am, *from* loss, *for* service, *in* suffering, *through* others, and *within* God.

What Does God Want? A Practical Guide to Making Decisions, Fr. Michael Scanlan, Franciscan University Press, 1996.

This highly practical book is written primarily for those seeking help in figuring out God's will for all kinds of decisions both small and large. Fr. Scanlan provides five criteria for ensuring that one's decisions are in conformity with God's will.

On Unique Motivational Design

The Power of Uniqueness: How to Become Who You Really Are, Arthur F. Miller, Jr. with William Hendricks, Zondervan, 1999.

This book is a full treatment of the phenomena, discovered by Miller, that a person's narrative of authentically satisfying action reveals a distinctive pattern of motivated behavior.